THE DIRECTORY OF
KNOTS

THE DIRECTORY OF
KNOTS

JOHN SHAW

ILLUSTRATED BY JOHN FOWLER

METRO BOOKS
NEW YORK

© 2003 THE IVY PRESS LIMITED
THIS 2009 EDITION PUBLISHED BY METRO BOOKS,
BY ARRANGEMENT WITH IVY PRESS

PUBLISHER'S NOTE
THIS BOOK IS A GENERAL INTRODUCTION TO THE USEFULNESS AND
PLEASURE OF KNOTTING. BEFORE USING ANY ONE OF THESE KNOTS, BENDS,
HITCHES, ETC. IN A POTENTIALLY HAZARDOUS SITUATION—WHETHER AT
WORK OR AT LEISURE—WITH FORESEEABLE RISKS OF INJURY, DAMAGE, OR
LOSS, YOU ARE STRONGLY ADVISED TO SEEK THE ADVICE AND TUITION OF
SUITABLY QUALIFIED PRACTITIONERS TO LEARN HOW TO TIE AND DEPLOY
THEM IN SUCH A SITUATION.

THIS BOOK WAS CONCEIVED, DESIGNED, AND PRODUCED BY
Ivy Press
THE OLD CANDLEMAKERS, WEST STREET,
LEWES, EAST SUSSEX, BN7 2NZ, UK

CREATIVE DIRECTOR PETER BRIDGEWATER
PUBLISHER SOPHIE COLLINS
EDITORIAL DIRECTOR STEVE LUCK
DESIGN MANAGER TONY SEDDON
DESIGNER TONWEN JONES
ILLUSTRATOR JOHN FOWLER
PROJECT EDITOR MANDY GREENFIELD

METRO BOOKS
122 FIFTH AVENUE
NEW YORK, NY 10011

ISBN-13: 978-1-4351-0811-0
ISBN-10: 1-4351-0811-6

PRINTED IN CHINA

10 9 8 7 6 5 4 3 2

CONTENTS

INTRODUCTION

Anyone can tie a knot or two . . . or the 100 (and more) contained in this book. If you cannot, it is merely because you have not yet learnt to do so. For knotting is one of those basic skills, like the ability to swim or read a map, that is accessible to all who choose to acquire them and separates self-sufficient and confident folk from the rest.

Tying knots is as satisfying as any other aspect of mental and manual dexterity, but has practical applications. In a new millennium that is likely to prove at least as hostile to humankind as the last one, knot tyers are among those helping to conserve the planet's dwindling and finite resources; for knots are reusable and, unlike factory-made and store-bought clips, clamps and other gadgets, come virtually free in terms of cash and energy consumption. And knot tying can be fun.

Today's knotting exponents – liberated from the survival needs for which our primitive ancestors first invented knots (to snare food, tote loads, erect shelters, tether animals and bind or even strangle enemies) – are free to indulge in a wider-ranging exploration of the fundamental but fascinating art, craft and science of knotting. For mathematicians there is the esoteric but rapidly growing postgraduate study of multidimensional knot theory; and, while there is no Nobel Prize for maths, its equivalent (the Field's Medal) was awarded in 1990 to the New Zealander Professor Vaughan Jones, F.R.S., for original contributions to this arcane subject.

Anglers, astronauts, cavers and climbers, conjurors, trappers, tree surgeons and wind surfers all know and use knots. They even invent new ones (some of which appear in this book). But you do not have to be an adventurous outdoor type, or a practitioner of some specialized skill, in order to benefit from knowing how to tie knots. You do not even have to like messing about in boats. Most knots are in fact tied by landlubbers, whether for leisure or for gain in cash and confidence, who find it an absorbing pursuit.

HELPFUL TERMS

Learning to tie knots and then practising them can be
done with a variety of stuff – which is the common term
used by knot tyers for cordage of all kinds (thin stuff,
thick stuff, expensive stuff, et cetera). More precisely,
anything over about 10 mm (⅜ inch) in diameter is
called a rope, while lesser diameters may be termed
braided cord, string or twine, according to their size,
construction and quality.

Rope that consists of three strands is known as a
hawser, but a rope that is made up of a number of
filaments enclosed in a braided outer covering is
(depending on the way it is made) said to be sheath-&-
core (kernmantel, in the case of climbing ropes) or braid-
on-braid construction. Any rope or cord with a specific
use is a line (for example, a towline, a washing line, a
heaving or throwing line).

Cordage manufactured in the age-old way from the
fibrous stems, leaves and seeds of plants includes
coir, cotton, flax, hemp and jute. The latest products,

however, comprise synthetic monofilaments and multifilaments that have been obtained mainly from the four Ps: polyamide (nylon), polyester (terylene or dacron), polypropylene and polyethylene (polythene). These durable manmade products are augmented by several so-called 'super or miracle fibres', such as Kevlar, which are marketed under various trade names.

The stuff that is sold in stores selling household goods will be cheaper by as much as a factor of 10 than the high-tech cordage stocked by ship chandlers or by climbing and camping suppliers. Indeed, because cordage can be costly, cut ends should always be heat-sealed, taped or seized with a length of thin twine to prevent waste from needless fraying or unravelling. However, all that is required to learn and practise the knots described in this book are two 2-m (6-foot) lengths of flexible, braided cord about 8 mm (⅓ inch) in diameter, preferably in two different colours so that the separate routes may be followed when tying two different lines together.

In all of the tying instructions that follow, the end that is actively involved in the tying process is referred to as the *working end*. The other end is known as the *standing end*, while that part of the rope or cord in between is known as the *standing part*. Any well defined U-shape within this standing part is called a *bight* and a bight may also be made by doubling over the working end.

Once a bight acquires a *crossing point* it becomes a *loop* and a couple of closely linked crossing points form *elbows*. A loop may be either overhand (when the working end is laid on top of the standing part) or underhand (when the working end is placed beneath the standing part). Knotted loops may be either fixed or adjustable (in other words, sliding), the latter commonly being called nooses. During the tying process some knots accumulate a series of unsecured knot parts resembling the rungs of a ladder. These must eventually be fixed in place by passing the working end between them, going alternately over, under, over, under; this is known as a *locking tuck*.

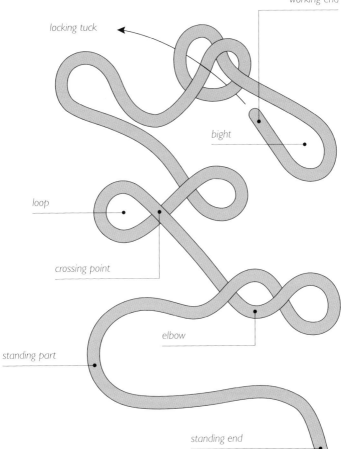

working end

locking tuck

bight

loop

crossing point

elbow

standing part

standing end

ON KNOTS IN GENERAL

The generic name for any cordage tie is a 'knot', but knots that join two lines together are identified as bends, while knots that attach a line to a rail, ring, post, or even another rope are known as hitches.

Strictly speaking, only something other than a bend or a hitch is a knot, including bindings, shortenings, stoppers and loops. There are exceptions. For instance, many loops make useful hitches since they can be cast on, off and on again, without the need to untie and retie them. And because earlier generations of seamen spoke of 'bending' any line to a ring, some ring hitches are actually called bends. Then again, bends and hitches primarily tied in small stuff, such as fishing line or package twine, are only ever referred to as knots.

Knots are the tools that make rope and other cordage work to justify its initial cost. Fortunately many are extremely versatile, all-purpose contrivances. The same knot, bend or hitch in rope might rescue someone from a mountain ledge or support a clothes line of freshly washed garments; yet, when tied in hair-thin nylon monofilament, it could be the means by which an angler lands a record-breaking fish. A stopper knot can prevent a rope block-&-tackle coming adrift or it can keep a sewing thread within the eye of a needle. It is just a matter of scale. Learn one knot, and you get at least another one free.

As a rule, knots weaken the cordage in which they occur. Knots tied quickly and simply are often the worst. Bulkier knots, with more wrapping turns, are stronger – that is, they reduce the breaking strength of line less drastically – but tying them may be trickier. So the selection of knot strength is a trade-off, a compromise between safety and convenience.

A knot may be strong, yet will slip and fall apart if tugged spasmodically or shaken, in which case it is insecure. Knot 'security' is a separate consideration from knot 'strength'. A knot must be both strong and secure enough for the job in hand.

SOME BASIC KNOTS

A few simple knots feature repeatedly on later pages of this book as component parts of other more elaborate knots, so they are introduced briefly here. The *overhand knot*, tied in the end of a rope or cord, is a basic stopper knot, an unsightly way of preventing the end of a length of line fraying, but a useful means of stopping it pulling out of a hole or slot.

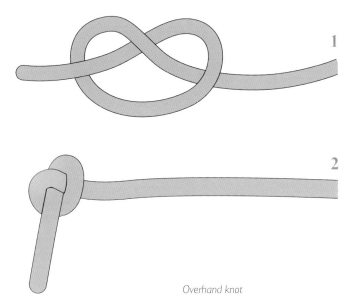

1

2

Overhand knot

The *figure-of-eight knot* is a better stopper knot than the overhand knot. Although it may appear to be bulkier, it does not actually have a greater diameter or block a bigger hole than the overhand knot. However, the figure-of-eight does having the advantage of being rather easier to untie after use, and is popular with knot-tyers because of its distinctive outline.

1

2

Figure-of-eight knot

When a drawloop (a bight made when the working end of the rope is not pulled completely through a knot) is added to the figure-of-eight, it becomes a *slipped figure-of-eight*. The drawloop ensures that the knot can always be untied by tugging on the working end. There is a case for using drawloops more frequently, since they do not weaken the knot – it is even possible that they may strengthen it.

Slipped figure-of-eight

When an overhand knot is rearranged around a rail, ring, rope or spar, it becomes a *half hitch*. However, when it is tied in both ends of the same line as a binding round or against something, it is referred to as a *half knot*.

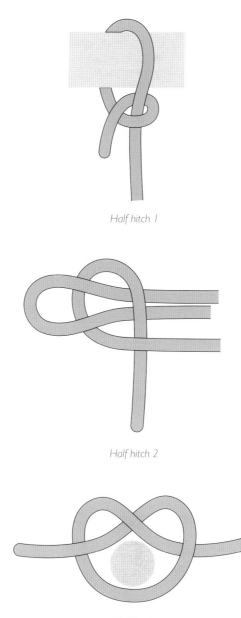

Half hitch 1

Half hitch 2

Half knot

Tuck the working end of an overhand knot a second time, pull gently on both ends to tighten it, and it twists and wraps round itself to create a *double overhand knot*.

Notice how the overhand, figure-of-eight and double overhand knots all change their shape when tightened. Many other knots do. Be amenable when a knot tells you what it wants to do – it usually knows best.

Double overhand knot

The world's favorite knots

THE WORLD'S FAVOURITE KNOTS

'Although there are thousands of different knots . . . there are a few knots which have proven their worth as the ones most generally useful.'

PERCY W. BLANDFORD, 1980

Watch those professionals who work with rope or smaller cordage and it soon becomes apparent that their knotting repertoire is restricted to a total of no more than perhaps ten knots, bends and hitches. Almost certainly they know more, and may use them in certain situations, but they routinely rely on a selection of general-purpose and time-honoured holdfasts.

INTRODUCTION

There are sensible reasons why those who tie a lot of knots tend to restrict their fingers to the same few tried-and-trusted ones. The need for any knot can arise at short notice, when it must be applied immediately, without time to consider which of several other alternatives might be preferable. Tying the knot itself should be done quickly, implying a practised familiarity with it. Then again, if the person who is tying the knot is one of a team or crew, it is essential that every member of that group can readily recognize and untie whatever has been previously applied by someone else. So the tyer must know that whatever he or she is tying will not later present the other members of the group with any sort of snag or difficulty.

Faced with the task of attaching a line to a rail, spar or post, generations of rope-workers have settled on the simple clove hitch (which can be tied by several differing methods) and its close relative the rolling hitch; and, for a ring hitch, on the round turn & two half hitches or its reliable cousin, the fisherman's bend.

To tie a fixed loop into the end of a line, often as a substitute for a hitch, our knotting ancestors relied upon a common bowline and its tougher variants, the water bowline and the double (or round turn) bowline. A simple adaptation of one or another of these – into a running bowline – served them well enough as a sliding noose.

To join two lines together they chose a basic sheet bend or, for more demanding jobs, the one-way and the double sheet bends. Meanwhile, in smaller stuff, the tendency was to employ a fisherman's knot (single, double or triple).

Reef knot

For odd jobs, a handy trio soon emerged: the reef knot, as a binding knot; the sheepshank, for a shortening; and the figure-of-eight stopper knot.

FIGURE-OF-EIGHT STOPPER KNOT

This knot is preferable to the overhand knot as a stopper, simply because it is easier to untie after use. Although bulkier, it will not fill a bigger hole. Tie it in the end of any rope that must remain within a pulley block or other item of rigging hardware.

Make a bight in the working end of the line and twist it around 180°, creating a loop (1).

Tuck the working end – over, under – down through the initial loop (2, 3).

Then tighten the knot (4), pulling down on the standing part of the line while holding the body of the knot stationary, until the end is bent almost at right angles to the standing part of the line.

ORIGIN
The nautical name for the figure-of-eight knot is Flemish knot, implying some kind of real or imagined western Germanic source.

SHEEPSHANK
TIED IN THE BIGHT

This oddly named knot is a basic shortening for a rope or cord that is too long for the job in hand, and too good to be cut to the required size. It works best with line that is hung vertically, because the knot (which is otherwise quite insecure) falls apart if no strain is placed upon it. Nevertheless it is a handy contrivance, readily tied in the bight.

Fold the spare standing part of the rope into three (making an S or Z shape), and slide an underhand loop over the upper bight (1, 2). This is sometimes known as a bellringer's knot, from its use in suspending surplus rope safely in a church belfry.

To complete the knot, add a similar half hitch to the lower bight (3).

ORIGIN

It is most unlikely this knot was ever used for tethering sheep so that they were restricted to grazing an area of grass defined by the length of the shortened rope that held them. The name is more likely to have come from the knot's resemblance to a sheep's legbone.

SHEEPSHANK
TIED WITH ENDS

The basic sheepshank tied in the bight (*see page 23*) is an
insecure knot that falls apart if not steadily loaded. Rarely
is a rope or cord so long that it must be made that way; and,
when either or both ends are accessible, it is better to tie
this wholly secure modification.

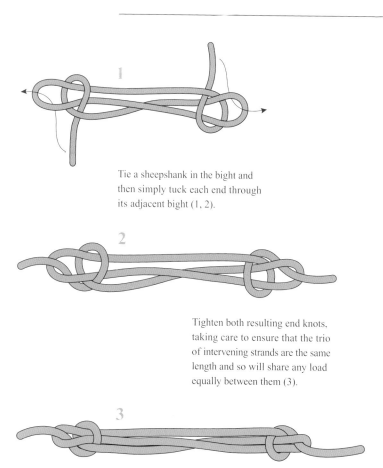

Tie a sheepshank in the bight and
then simply tuck each end through
its adjacent bight (1, 2).

Tighten both resulting end knots,
taking care to ensure that the trio
of intervening strands are the same
length and so will share any load
equally between them (3).

CLOVE HITCH TIED WITH AN END

This classic hitch can be rapidly applied and just as quickly taken apart again. It resembles a letter N (or its mirror-image, if the knot is tied the other way round). As long as the strain on it is more or less at right angles to the anchorage point, it will hold well enough; but it will loosen, slip and may come adrift if pulled or tugged askew.

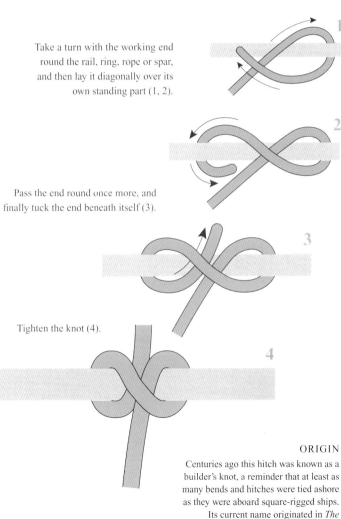

Take a turn with the working end round the rail, ring, rope or spar, and then lay it diagonally over its own standing part (1, 2).

Pass the end round once more, and finally tuck the end beneath itself (3).

Tighten the knot (4).

ORIGIN

Centuries ago this hitch was known as a builder's knot, a reminder that at least as many bends and hitches were tied ashore as they were aboard square-rigged ships. Its current name originated in *The Universal Dictionary of the Marine* (1769) by William Falconer.

CLOVE HITCH
TIED IN THE BIGHT

Tying any knot 'in the bight' generally results in a more fluent manipulation, and this knot is no exception to the rule. In addition, it brings about dynamic control of whatever is loading the standing part of the line.

1

Cast an underhand loop (that is, one in which the line nearest the end goes beneath the standing part) and place it over the post, stanchion, tree stump or whatever else is to be the anchorage point (1).

2

Use the friction generated by this turn to control, slow and stop the load. Adjust the standing part to the required length and then add a second underhand loop to complete and secure the knot (2, 3).

3

Rolling hitch

Closely related to the clove hitch (*see pages 25 and 26*),
this descendant evolved to cope with a longitudinal pull
of any kind.

Pass the working end round the
object and take a diagonal turn
with it across the standing part (1).

Make a second identical turn,
fitting it snugly between the first
one and the standing part (2).
Then finish off with a half hitch
on the other side of the knot (3).

Work the knot snug and tight (4). The
pull must be made on the side of the
knot supported by the twin turns, so
there is a 50:50 chance whether this
version or its mirror-image is required.

ORIGIN

The name rolling hitch emerged around
1841. Older knotting manuals refer to it
as the Magnus hitch or Magner's hitch,
and today there is disagreement as to
whether or not this was merely an earlier
name for the same knot or if those names
referred to the alternative way of tying it.

ROUND TURN & TWO HALF HITCHES

Use this secure alternative to the clove hitch (*see pages 25 and 26*) when that knot is likely to prove inadequate. The round turn adds strength and supports the weight of the load; the two half hitches hold it in position.

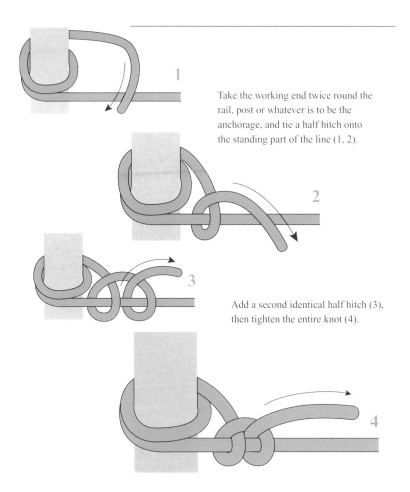

Take the working end twice round the rail, post or whatever is to be the anchorage, and tie a half hitch onto the standing part of the line (1, 2).

Add a second identical half hitch (3), then tighten the entire knot (4).

ORIGIN

This knot may be of enormous age and antiquity, although the name for it first appeared in *Elements & Practice of Rigging and Seamanship* (1794) by David Steel.

FISHERMAN'S BEND

This knot is taught for its use with wet anchor warps, which can become slimed with seaweed, at which point the round turn & two half hitches (*see opposite*) could slip and even come undone. This modification should be employed whenever a more secure hitch is required.

Take a complete round turn with the working end, like a forwards somersault, through the ring (1).

Then pass it behind the standing part and through the turn, to trap the initial half hitch (2).

Add a second identical half hitch and tighten the knot (3, 4).

ORIGIN

It is because seamen in the days of merchant and naval sailing ships always spoke of 'bending' a rope to a ring that this hitch is called the fisherman's bend or the anchor bend.

BOWLINE

The most common uses for a simple fixed loop like this one are either to start lashings and package ties or as a smartly applied and equally smartly cast-off hitch to a post.

Make an overhand loop (that is, one in which the line nearest to the working end lies on top) and tuck the end up through it, under, then over (1, 2).

Pass the end round behind the standing part and then tuck it down through the initial loop (3).

Tighten the knot, and secure the loose end by means of a double overhand knot round the nearest loop leg (4).

ORIGIN

The name (pronounced 'boh-linn') is a corruption of 'bow line' and was used to refer to a rope that ran from the forwards end of a ship to a square-sail yard, in certain sailing attitudes, so as to prevent it being accidentally taken aback (that is, blown inside out).

WATER BOWLINE

The common bowline (*see opposite*) can spill when tied
in stiff or slippery line. This variation is just as strong
but more secure, and will withstand being towed through
water or dragged over rough ground.

Form an overhand loop (that is, one
in which the working end lies on
top of the standing part), then add a
second identical one beneath it (1).

Tuck the working end up through
each loop in turn, pass it round
the standing part, then tuck it back
down through both loops (2).

Tighten the knot in two stages, starting
with the first loop. Then slide the second
loop up to join its companion (3).

DOUBLE ROUND TURN BOWLINE

The bowline, despite its pedigree, is not particularly strong or very secure. If these qualities are crucial to the knot's performance, use this tougher version instead, although being able to tie the common bowline (*see page 30*) will render this one easier.

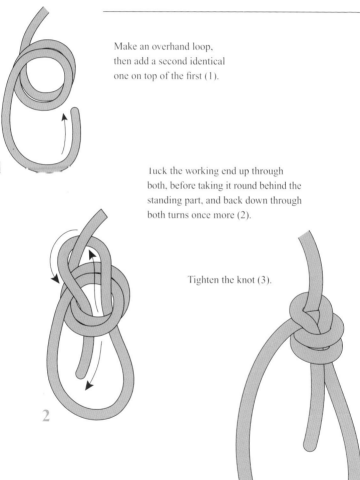

Make an overhand loop, then add a second identical one on top of the first (1).

Tuck the working end up through both, before taking it round behind the standing part, and back down through both turns once more (2).

Tighten the knot (3).

Running bowline

This is a quick and simple free-running noose to make. It closes readily round whatever it contains, but cannot jam and is therefore just as easily released.

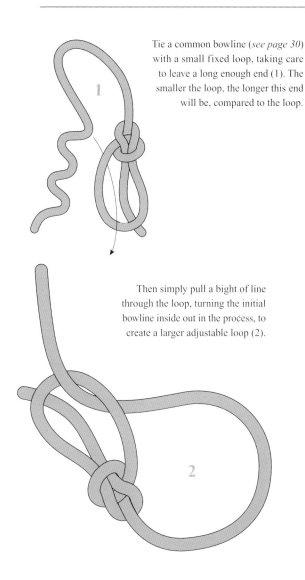

Tie a common bowline (*see page 30*) with a small fixed loop, taking care to leave a long enough end (1). The smaller the loop, the longer this end will be, compared to the loop.

Then simply pull a bight of line through the loop, turning the initial bowline inside out in the process, to create a larger adjustable loop (2).

REEF OR SQUARE KNOT

Use of this knot really must be limited to packages, first aid and other small-scale items. It is a binding knot, usually tied in both ends of the same length of material, which relies for its security on being pressed against something (shoelace upon foot, bandage to limb, hair ribbon round plait, et cetera). But, as all knotting is a trade-off between convenience and reliability, plenty of occasions arise when this is all that is needed.

Tie a simple half knot – left-over-right (1).

Then add a second half knot of the opposite handedness – right-over-left (2, 3).

Tug firmly on either both ends, at the same time, to tighten the resulting knot (4).

ORIGIN

The European name for this knot comes from its use on older sailboats for reefing sail, by folding or rolling lower sections of canvas and then securing them with a pair of cordage reefing points. The knot was known to the ancient Romans as the Hercules knot.

SHEET BEND

This layout has already been encountered in the common bowline (*see page 30*), but in this altered configuration joins two lines of slightly differing size or construction. A sheet bend should be tied so that both short ends occur on the same side, because the so-called 'left-handed' version (with the ends on opposite sides) can in some cordage be less secure.

Make a bight in the end of the larger or stiffer line (1).

Insert the working end of the other line, pass it round behind and beneath both legs of the bight, and then tuck it beneath itself (2, 3).

Tighten the knot (4).

ORIGIN

The name comes from its use in 'bending' ropes to sails (sheets), and it was featured in *Elements & Practice of Rigging & Seamanship* (1794) by David Steel; but Neolithic people used a knot with an identical layout to tie the meshes of fishing nets.

ONE-WAY SHEET BEND

The common sheet bend has the slight disadvantage that
one end projects at right angles to the knot. If that could
snag – for instance, when pulling the joined lines over or
through a narrow gap – use this streamlined version instead.

Tie a common sheet bend (*see page
35*) and then tuck the working end
back beneath its own standing part (1).

Tighten the knot so that three parts
lie snugly together, all pointing in
the same direction (2).

The common sheet bend (*see page 35*) can spill, if the
lines that it joins are greatly dissimilar in either size or
construction. If you are in any doubt, use the double
sheet bend instead.

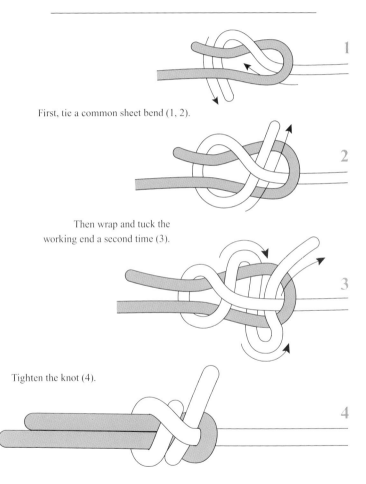

First, tie a common sheet bend (1, 2).

Then wrap and tuck the
working end a second time (3).

Tighten the knot (4).

FISHERMAN'S KNOT

Despite its misleading name, this knot – when tied in rope – is actually a bend. It is more secure than a sheet bend, but should be tied only in lines of the same size or construction.

Lay the two lines together, parallel, with the working ends opposed (1).

With one end, tie an overhand knot around the other standing part (2).

Repeat the process with the other end, making sure that both knots are of identical handedness – if one spirals anticlockwise (as shown), then so must the other (3).

Tighten the two knots, then pull on the standing parts to slide them together (4).

ORIGIN

As the convention is that bends and hitches tied in small stuff are simply called 'knots', the name of this knot presumably originated with medieval anglers and was tied in fishing lines of horsehair or gut.

DOUBLE FISHERMAN'S KNOT

More wrapping turns imbue a knot with greater strength and make it more secure, which is why this bulked-up version of the fisherman's knot (*see opposite*) is popular with climbers and cavers, who use it to create endless slings or strops. It is not easily undone, however, once it has been heavily loaded.

Lay the two lines alongside one another, parallel, with the ends opposed (1).

With one end, tie a double overhand knot round the other standing part (2).

Repeat the process with the other end, ensuring that both knots have the same handedness – if one spirals anticlockwise (as shown), then so must the other (3).

Tighten both knots, then pull on the standing ends to slide them together (4).

ORIGIN

The basic fisherman's knot is unsuitable for most modern nylon fishing lines, but the doubled version is employed by anglers, who know it as the grinner knot, presumably because of the smiley mouth made with the two lines between the knots while they remain apart.

TRIPLE FISHERMAN'S KNOT

For still greater strength and security, anglers and climbers in particular favour this muscle-bound version of the basic knot, which anglers call a double grinner knot.

Lay the two lines alongside one another, parallel, with the ends opposed. With one working end, tie a triple overhand knot round the other standing part (1, 2).

Repeat the process with the other end, ensuring that both knots have the same handedness – if one spirals anticlockwise (as shown), then so must the other. Tighten both knots, then pull on the standing ends to slide them together (3).

20 PRACTICAL KNOTS

Knots make rope work and, while it is possible to use (and sometimes to misuse or abuse) the same old ones for every task that comes along, having a wider repertoire literally at one's fingertips is a better strategy.

INTRODUCTION

Learning to tie any knot is easier when you know what the completed knot looks like, so this book includes both step-by-step tying stages and an image of the tied and tightened knot. There is, however, more than one way to tie most knots, and in *The Directory of Knots* the one that is depicted is generally just the method considered easiest to learn, or in some cases the one that could be most clearly illustrated. Learn it – you will certainly not be wasting your time.

Here is a tip that can lead to discovering another quicker and more fluent tying method for some knots. Some hitches, when removed from their rail, post or other anchoring foundation, fall apart until nothing of them remains. Examples in this section are the pole hitch and the cat's paw. And some loops, if a retaining bight is withdrawn from them, also collapse and vanish. The angler's loop is a prime example. Knots like this, which can (to put it pedantically) be 'untied in the bight' can also be tied 'in the bight' – that is, without using either end of the line. Applying this test can reveal a distinct difference between knots that otherwise are only a tuck or turn apart in their make-up. For instance, the constrictor knot can be tied in the bight, but the strangle knot cannot; and untying in the bight often instructs you in how to tie the knot in the bight.

This previously unsuspected relationship was identified and defined as the Law of Loop, Hitch & Bight by Dr Harry Asher, MA, PhD, who first published it in *A New System of Knotting* (1986) and later in his *Alternative Knot Book* (1989). Tying a knot in the bight can be a quick and efficient (almost sleight-of-hand) method, with the obvious advantage that it can be done even when neither end of the line is accessible. It is always worth learning to do.

Constrictor knot tied in the bight

STEVEDORE KNOT

Dock workers whose livelihood involved hoisting and moving loads by means of simple block-&-tackle used this knot in preference to the basic figure-of-eight stopper (*see page 22*). It does not block a bigger hole, but is bulkier and easier to untie when the rope must be continually removed from one pulley to another.

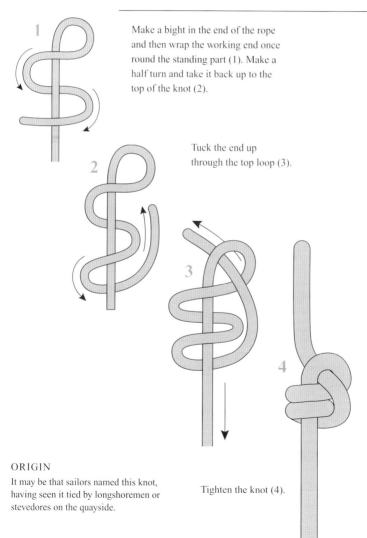

Make a bight in the end of the rope and then wrap the working end once round the standing part (1). Make a half turn and take it back up to the top of the knot (2).

Tuck the end up through the top loop (3).

Tighten the knot (4).

ORIGIN

It may be that sailors named this knot, having seen it tied by longshoremen or stevedores on the quayside.

difference between knots that otherwise are only a tuck or turn apart in their make-up. For instance, the constrictor knot can be tied in the bight, but the strangle knot cannot; and untying in the bight often instructs you in how to tie the knot in the bight.

This previously unsuspected relationship was identified and defined as the Law of Loop, Hitch & Bight by Dr Harry Asher, MA, PhD, who first published it in *A New System of Knotting* (1986) and later in his *Alternative Knot Book* (1989). Tying a knot in the bight can be a quick and efficient (almost sleight-of-hand) method, with the obvious advantage that it can be done even when neither end of the line is accessible. It is always worth learning to do.

Constrictor knot tied in the bight

STEVEDORE KNOT

Dock workers whose livelihood involved hoisting and moving loads by means of simple block-&-tackle used this knot in preference to the basic figure-of-eight stopper (*see page 22*). It does not block a bigger hole, but is bulkier and easier to untie when the rope must be continually removed from one pulley to another.

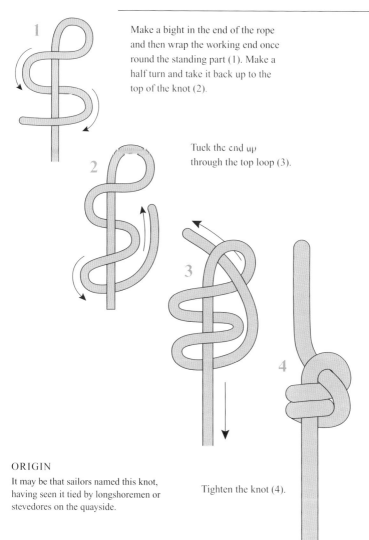

Make a bight in the end of the rope and then wrap the working end once round the standing part (1). Make a half turn and take it back up to the top of the knot (2).

Tuck the end up through the top loop (3).

Tighten the knot (4).

ORIGIN

It may be that sailors named this knot, having seen it tied by longshoremen or stevedores on the quayside.

When the figure-of-eight and stevedore stopper knots prove inadequate, enabling the rope in which they are tied to pull free, then use this chunky alternative. Originally called the oysterman's stopper knot, it has now become a favourite with knot tyers and a minor classic.

Tie a slipped overhand knot or simple noose, and tighten it (1, 2).

Take the short end round the standing part and tuck it through the loop (3).

Pull down on the standing part to shrink the loop and trap the end (4).

ORIGIN

This knot was devised by American book illustrator and author Clifford Warren Ashley more than 90 years ago. Having spotted a knot he could not identify aboard an oyster-fishing boat, this was his attempt to reproduce it, although he later found it to be merely a figure-of-eight knot.

STRANGLE KNOT

This alternative to the constrictor knot (*see opposite*) is preferred by some knot tyers because the turns bed-down more snugly; but, unlike the constrictor, it cannot be tied in the bight. The strangle knot is actually a double overhand knot tied loosely, then slipped over and round something (rope's end, sack neck, roll of wallpaper) as a ligature, instead of as a mere stopper knot.

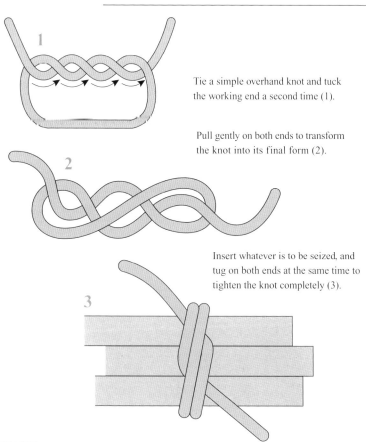

Tie a simple overhand knot and tuck the working end a second time (1).

Pull gently on both ends to transform the knot into its final form (2).

Insert whatever is to be seized, and tug on both ends at the same time to tighten the knot completely (3).

ORIGIN

This is one of several so-called sack or miller's knots that were once required to tie off the flax, jute or hessian bags that our ancestors used to hold bushels or pecks of grain, seed, flour and other staple commodities produced by windmills and the later factories.

CONSTRICTOR KNOT
TIED WITH AN END

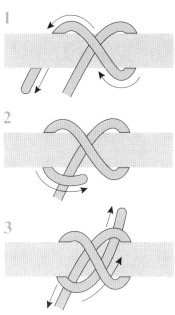

This is probably the world's best seizing knot, so secure that it has to be cut off after use. It makes a rapid first-aid tourniquet for the cut end of a rope, to prevent it fraying and unravelling, which can be left in place to become a semi-permanent binding. It will also hold a hosepipe on a tap, clamp woodwork while glue dries or attach pencil to string for use on a clipboard.

Pass the working end of a length of cord or twine round the item to be bound, then cross it diagonally over the initial turn (1).

Take the end once more round the foundation, and then tuck it over (the standing part), under, under, as shown (2, 3).

Pull strongly on both ends to tighten this knot, using pliers or other aids for the tightest possible grip (4).

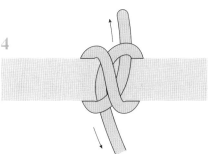

To remove the knot, sever the overriding diagonal knot part. The knot will fall away in two cut segments, without damage to whatever lay beneath it.

ORIGIN

This knot is believed to be one of 18 described (but not illustrated) in a brief essay on surgical slings by the Greek physician Heraklas, in the first century AD. It may also have been the so-called gunner's knot, and was used as a whip knot by Spanish muleteers in the 1930s.

CONSTRICTOR KNOT
WITH DRAWLOOP

Although the constrictor is essentially a semi-permanent seizing, it can also be resorted to as the most temporary of holdfasts, in which case it makes sense to tie it without pulling the working end completely through the knot. The result is a drawloop that can later be used to release the knot – no knife needed.

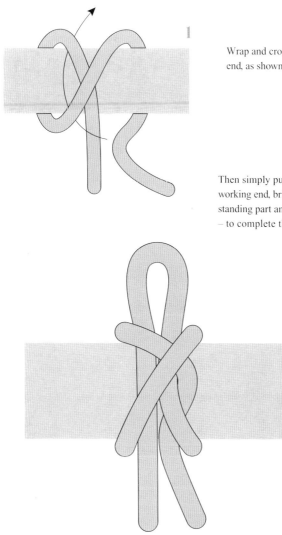

Wrap and cross the working end, as shown (1).

Then simply pull a bight from the working end, bring it in front of the standing part and tuck – under, under – to complete the knot (2). Tighten.

CONSTRICTOR KNOT TIED IN THE BIGHT

When it can be done, tying any knot 'in the bight' (that is to say, without using either end of the line) is invariably quicker. Indeed, the dexterity engendered is almost sleight of hand. So, when the end of the rope, hosepipe or other item to be seized is accessible, tie the basic constrictor knot this way.

Take a turn with the working end and pull out a bight from the lower part (1).

Bring it round and across the other knot parts to pass over the end of the foundation (2, 3).

Tighten the knot in the usual manner (4).

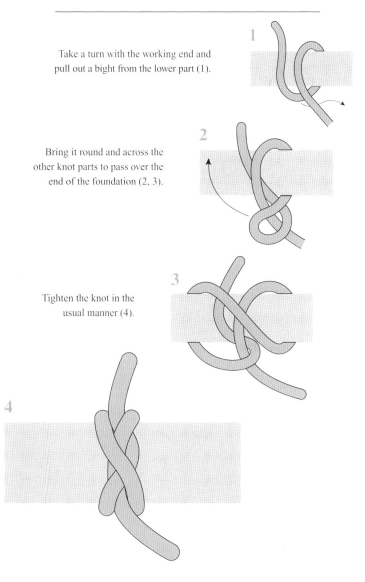

DOUBLE CONSTRICTOR KNOT TIED WITH AN END

You can employ this reinforced version of the basic constrictor knot in any situation where the reliability of the latter may be doubtful.

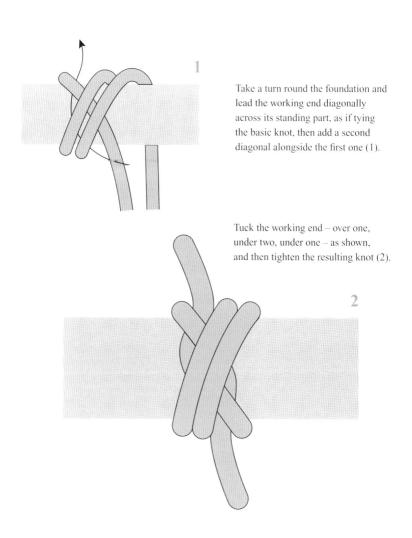

1

Take a turn round the foundation and lead the working end diagonally across its standing part, as if tying the basic knot, then add a second diagonal alongside the first one (1).

Tuck the working end – over one, under two, under one – as shown, and then tighten the resulting knot (2).

2

DOUBLE CONSTRICTOR KNOT TIED IN THE BIGHT

Tying in the bight is always preferable and, provided the end of the item to be seized is accessible, the double constrictor knot can be achieved this way.

First, tie a clove hitch (*see page 25*), then pull out a bight from behind the upper loose end (1, 2).

Wrap the bight down and round, passing over the end of the foundation, to create a second diagonal alongside the first one (3).

Tighten the knot (4).

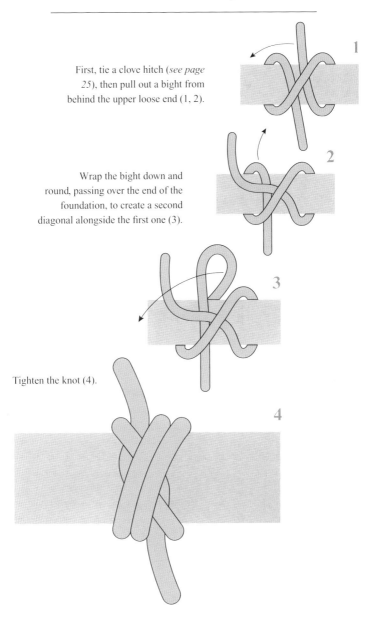

POLE HITCH

For making and carrying bundles (ranging from garden trellis stakes to sailboat masts and spars), a pair of these knots is unbeatable.

Lay out the lashing in an S or Z shape and place the items to be lashed together on top (1).

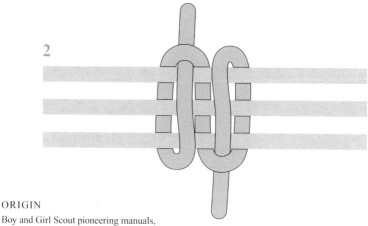

ORIGIN

Boy and Girl Scout pioneering manuals, more than any other, have preserved the knowledge of this knot.

Tuck each end of the line through the opposite bight (2).

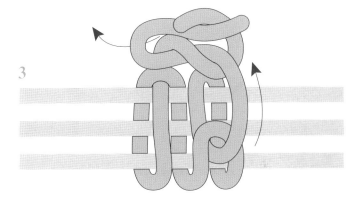

3

Then pull up on both ends to wrap
the twin bights firmly round the
load they now contain (3).

Lastly, tie off the two ends with a reef
or square knot (4). Add a second pole
hitch at the other end of long items.

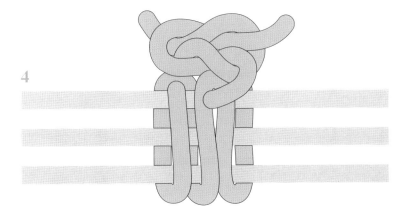

4

Buntline hitch

When a line is attached to a ring or other item of hardware that is likely to be continually shaken or otherwise disturbed (for example, when tied to a sail or flag halyard), use this secure, yet compact knot. Because the short end is trapped against the anchorage point, it is unlikely to come loose, although that can also make it awkward to untie. It is dual-purpose, however, working equally well in cordage or flat webbing.

Pass the working end through the ring or other point of attachment, then wrap and tuck it, as shown (1, 2, 3). The result is a clove hitch (*see page 25*) tied round the standing part of the line.

Tighten the knot itself, and then slide it up snug against the ring (4).

1

2

3

4

ORIGIN

Buntlines were ropes that hung loose from a ship's topsails, where they were subjected to severe wind disturbance, and so only a secure knot would do to attach them. When the necktie superseded the cravat as an item of wear, this was the knot taught by generations of fathers to sons.

OSSEL HITCH

This resilient little hitch was frequently used by sea fisherman to suspend their driftnets from short vertical lengths of cord. It had to cope with being tugged about by underwater movement and proved a reliable, yet simple knot for the job.

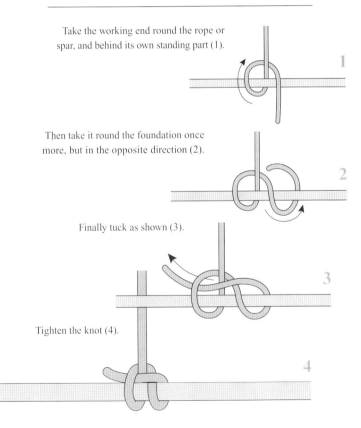

Take the working end round the rope or spar, and behind its own standing part (1).

Then take it round the foundation once more, but in the opposite direction (2).

Finally tuck as shown (3).

Tighten the knot (4).

ORIGIN

The word 'ossel' (or sometimes 'orsel') is a British regional version of 'norsel' (for the length of cord that connects gill nets to their head-ropes).

OSSEL KNOT

The ossel knot is a kissing cousin of the ossel hitch (*see page 55*), but is employed as a fishing knot closer to the surface of the sea than its relative. There conditions are rougher and so it must be more robust.

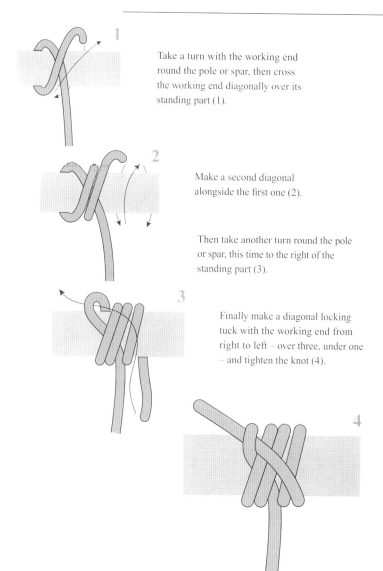

Take a turn with the working end round the pole or spar, then cross the working end diagonally over its standing part (1).

Make a second diagonal alongside the first one (2).

Then take another turn round the pole or spar, this time to the right of the standing part (3).

Finally make a diagonal locking tuck with the working end from right to left – over three, under one – and tighten the knot (4).

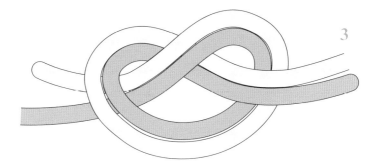

3

Rearrange the initial layout, if necessary, so that the load falling upon the standing parts is exerted at the outside ends of the knot (4) – it is stronger that way. If the standing parts cross directly at the heart of the knot, then in time they could chafe or saw through one another.

4

FIGURE-OF-EIGHT BEND

This is a fairly strong bend that, depending on the stuff in which it is tied, is generally easier to untie than the water knot (*see pages 60–61*). Unlike that versatile knot, it is unsuitable for tape or webbing.

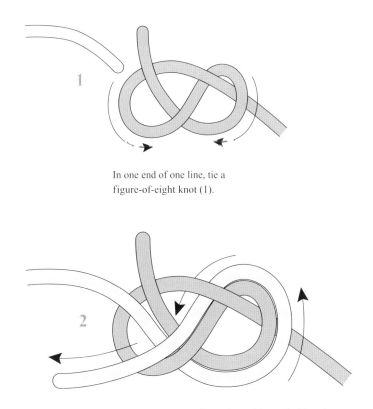

In one end of one line, tie a figure-of-eight knot (1).

Insert the working end of the other line, and follow the initial lead round to reproduce the knot (2, 3).

ORIGIN

Just as the figure-of-eight stopper knot (*see page 22*) was once known as the Flemish knot, so this was called the Flemish bend.

Then begin to tighten the knot (3).

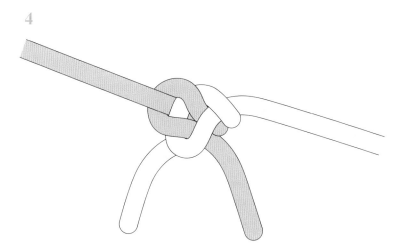

Let the knot capsize into its final form
(4), which is unrecognizable
from the initial layout.

However, the knot is found as a
decorative motif in the much earlier
Elizabethan plasterwork of Ormonde
Castle at Carrick-on-Suir, Ireland. Earlier
still, it was the badge of the rebel English
leader Hereward the Wake, who opposed
William the Conqueror in 1070; and it is
still occasionally called the Wake knot.

ZEPPELIN BEND

There is an entire family of bends made up from a couple of interlocked overhand knots, of which this is the easiest to tie right every time. It is also a proven workhorse (*see Origin below*).

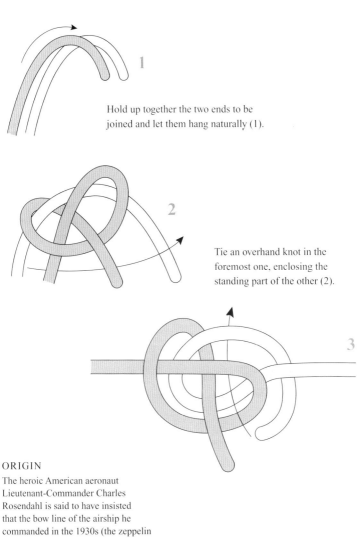

1

Hold up together the two ends to be joined and let them hang naturally (1).

2

Tie an overhand knot in the foremost one, enclosing the standing part of the other (2).

3

ORIGIN

The heroic American aeronaut Lieutenant-Commander Charles Rosendahl is said to have insisted that the bow line of the airship he commanded in the 1930s (the zeppelin *Los Angeles*) was attached to her ground mooring lines with this knot.

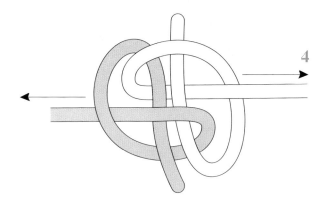

Then bring that standing part forwards and
tuck its working end up through the central
compartments made by both strands (3, 4).

Tighten the knot (5).

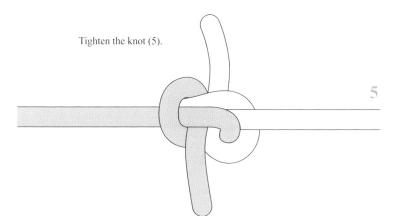

The knot remained in use by the US
Navy until 1962 for securing lighter-
than-air craft – those instructors who
knew its history referred to it as the
Rosendahl bend. Two journalists, Bob
and Lee Payne, assigned it the Z-word in
an article for *Boating* magazine in 1976.

ANGLER'S LOOP

This all-purpose fixed loop works perfectly (its other name is the perfection loop) in rope, cord, twine and some fishing lines. It even captures and holds bungee cord, which wriggles free from many otherwise dependable knots.

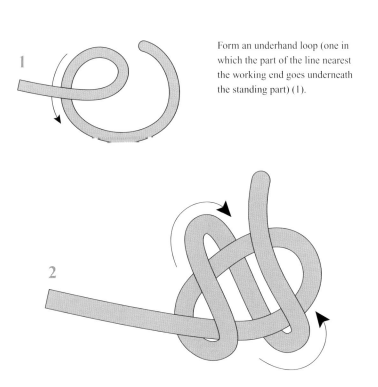

Form an underhand loop (one in which the part of the line nearest the working end goes underneath the standing part) (1).

Then wrap the end completely round both legs of the loop, as shown (2).

ORIGIN

This is an age-old angling knot, a survivor from the days of horsehair and gut fishing lines. At one time it was viewed with disfavour by rope workers because it would jam in vegetable-fibre cordage. In today's synthetic ropes and cords, however, it is ideal.

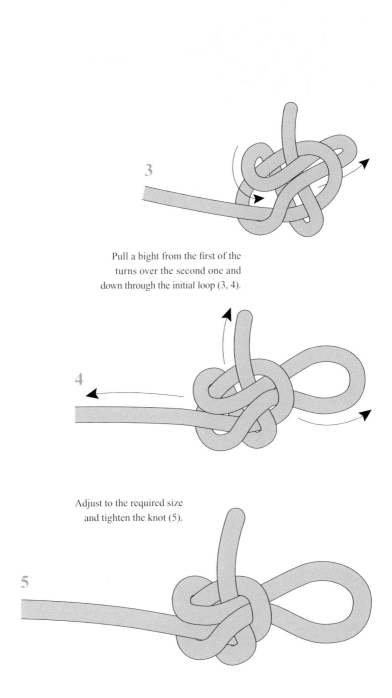

3

Pull a bight from the first of the
turns over the second one and
down through the initial loop (3, 4).

4

Adjust to the required size
and tighten the knot (5).

5

MIDSHIPMAN'S LOOP

This is one of those slide-&-grip loop knots, useful when tent guylines, laundry lines and such like must be slackened off or tightened to cope with varying conditions. In the artisan's workshop and the artist's studio it has also proved its worth for suspending bits and pieces, when two hands prove insufficient.

Pass the end round, through or over the rail, ring, post or other anchorage point and make an overhand loop (one in which that part of the line nearest the working end goes over the standing part) (1).

1

Tuck the end through the loop, lay it diagonally over itself, then insert a second similar diagonal snugly between the first one and the upper loop leg (2, 3).

2

ORIGIN
The name implies use aboard naval warships during the days of sail, when a midshipman was a more senior or experienced rank than the junior one it became in modern times.

3

Lastly, add a retaining half hitch above the standing part (4).

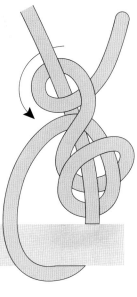

4

Tighten the knot, carefully eliminating all of the slack, so that what results is in effect a rolling hitch (*see page 27*) that slides (5). The knot may be shifted readily enough by hand to alter the size of the loop; but, when loaded, it will hold firm.

5

BOWLINE IN THE BIGHT

Twin fixed loops can be used to spread a load or share it between two separate anchorage points. This variation of the common bowline (*see page 30*) has the advantage that it can be tied in the bight.

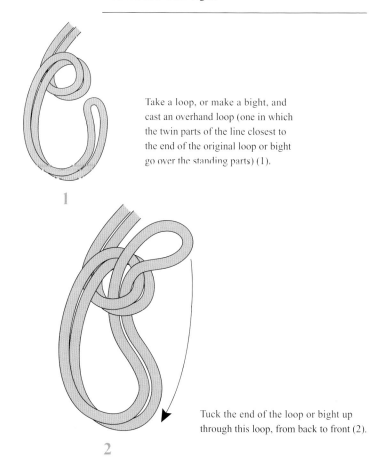

Take a loop, or make a bight, and cast an overhand loop (one in which the twin parts of the line closest to the end of the original loop or bight go over the standing parts) (1).

1

Tuck the end of the loop or bight up through this loop, from back to front (2).

2

ORIGIN

Like many other twin-loop knots, the bowline in the bight almost certainly came into existence as an improvised chair knot in which a workman sat suspended – one loop beneath his thighs, the other round his chest and armpits – to work up masts, down wells, etc.

Assuming that the standing parts of
the line are too long to tuck through in
the usual way, bend the bight down in
front of the uncompleted knot and
pass the two large loops through it (3).

3

Then lift the bight up once more behind
the standing parts (4). This knot almost
tightens itself, but should be made snug
by hand before use. See how the entire
knot is doubled, except for the retaining
bight round the standing parts,
which remains single.

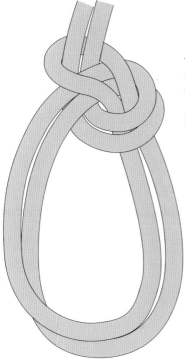

4

In these more safety-conscious
and litigious times, such use is not
recommended; approved safety harnesses
should be preferred. Nevertheless, in an
emergency when nothing else is available,
a knowledge of such knots may
still prove invaluable.

TOM FOOL'S KNOT

The name of this knot implies – wrongly – that it is somehow weak, impractical and not to be used. In fact, a study in 1996 by British professional firefighter Colin Grundy, of rope-chair rescue knots, determined that it was equal in effectiveness to the generally preferred handcuff knot on the opposite page.

Form an alternating pair of loops, one overhand, the other underhand, and overlap them as shown (1).

Then simply pull a bight from the right-hand loop through the left-hand loop, and vice versa (2).

Pull on the lower loop legs to adjust them to the required size, then pull on the upper loop legs to tighten the knot (3).

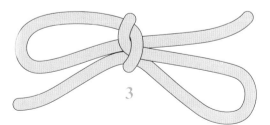

ORIGIN

In the various British fire brigades, this knot has been the basis for an emergency human-rescue knot since the chair knot (as it is known to everyone else), was introduced by the Victorian chief officer, Eyre Massey-Shaw, in 1876.

Handcuff knot

Unlike the bowline in the bight (*see pages 72–73*),
this knot (which is liked by young knot tyers because it
challenges their abilities as would-be escape artists) has
adjustable loops.

Make a couple of overhand loops
and overlap them, as shown (1).

Pull a bight from the upper loop down
through the lower one, and vice versa (2).

Adjust the loops to the required
size and tighten the knot (3).

To lock each loop in position, tie
a half hitch round it with the
adjacent standing part (4).

ORIGIN

It is most likely that so-called handcuff
knots actually evolved to hobble animals,
leting them graze over a limited area, but
preventing them straying too far from
overnight campsites. They also have a
history as emergency chair knots, used in
particular by fire rescue services.

LAPP KNOT

Knots that incorporate a drawloop as a quick-release can often leave fingers and fingernails with a final bit of untying. The Lapp knot is pure escapism: tug the short end and it falls apart. Unjustly dismissed by some as a 'false' sheet bend, this knot has in fact been known for at least a century.

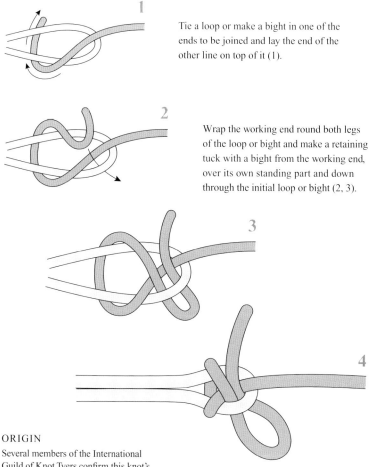

Tie a loop or make a bight in one of the ends to be joined and lay the end of the other line on top of it (1).

Wrap the working end round both legs of the loop or bight and make a retaining tuck with a bight from the working end, over its own standing part and down through the initial loop or bight (2, 3).

ORIGIN

Several members of the International Guild of Knot Tyers confirm this knot's distinct and discrete identity. In the Guild's April 1996 issue of *Knotting Matters*, Robert Pont of France reported having seen it used in Lapland to secure knife lanyards and hitch reindeer to sleds.

Carefully tighten the knot into a stable and secure, compact form (4).

Traditional knots

TRADITIONAL KNOTS

There is a generous legacy of knots bequeathed to us by

our ancestors, who employed them in multifarious ways.

Wilderness pioneers lashed loads to pack animals, bucketed

water from wells and probed the earth for ores and oil.

The first large buildings were erected using rope tackles and

lashed scaffolding, and on a smaller scale individual farmers

and storekeepers, shoe menders, bookbinders and weavers

all relied upon a much-used knot or two. A selection of these

time-honoured (and never outmoded) knots follows.

INTRODUCTION

Whether a knot is tied 'in the bight' (that is, without using either end of the line) or not, the working end can often either be pulled completely through the finished knot or left protruding in the form of a small bight, known as a drawloop. Knots with drawloops are termed 'slipped-knots'.

A drawloop does not, it must be stressed, convert any knot into a life-saving, quick-release hitch (such as the Lapp knot on page 76). It merely ensures that the knot incorporating it can be undone without breaking fingernails in the process. Nevertheless, drawloops ought to be used more than they currently are, since they do not weaken the knots in which they appear. In fact, they may actually strengthen them by the inclusion of an extra section of rope or cord. Security will not be increased and may, depending upon what knot and what material are used, actually be reduced somewhat; but, as knots are more often than not tight enough for what they are required to do, that may be no bad thing. Examples of traditional knots with drawloops in this section are the ground line hitch and the horse dealer's hitch.

The drawloop is just one instance of a phenomenon that a periodic contributor to *Knotting Matters*, writing under the pen-name Cy Canute, described in September 2000 as the 'parsimonious' – in other words, economical, mean or stingy – nature of knotting.

Ground line hitch with drawloop

Other instances of this parsimony principle are: that bowlines and sheet bends have similar layouts, so learn one and the other comes virtually free in terms of time and effort; adjustable nooses are commonly locked by the addition of half hitches; many traditional knots have as their basis the overhand and figure-of-eight knots; and bulky knots with lots of wrapping turns (collectively referred to as 'blood knots') can usually be reckoned very strong knots. Be alert for such shared features and a large repertoire of interrelated knots will be more easily acquired.

GOOD-LUCK OR SHAMROCK LANYARD KNOT

A lanyard is a short length of cord, attached to a belt or hung round the neck, to retain anything from a knife or stopwatch to a lucky charm. Lanyard knots serve either to form a retaining loop for whatever is to be attached to the cord, to embellish it, or (as in this case) to do both at once.

Double the length of cord and pull out three finger-like bights (1).

Pick up the two standing parts and lay them to the right, over the adjacent bight. Place this bight over the next bight, continuing anticlockwise. Then put the second bight across the third, and make a locking tuck with the third beneath the twin loops created by the initial move (2).

ORIGIN

This knot is one of the simplest in an ancient Oriental series of increasingly elaborate crown knots, but was named only as recently as 1981 by knotting writer Lydia Chen in her book *Chinese Knotting*.

Gradually work this crown knot, as it is called, snug. Pull each knot part in turn to eliminate all the unwanted slack. Take care that pairs of strands lie parallel – like rail tracks – and do not twist or cross each other. Then, *without turning the work over*, start making a clockwise crown knot (3).

Follow the same procedure as
before, placing each bight over the
adjacent bight, but this time
working in a clockwise direction (4).

Tighten this second stage, adjusting the three
primary loops to the required size, and (as
optional ornamentation) create four smaller
secondary loops in the final knot (5).

If you start with four bights instead
of three, then a five-part shamrock
knot may also be tied (6).

CHINESE LANYARD KNOT

This ornamental knot is simpler to tie than it appears on the printed page, although tightening to achieve the unusual square outline requires care and patience. But nothing ventured, nothing gained.

Double a length of cord and, leaving a bight, tie a pair of matching half knots. After a gap, tie a similar pair of half knots (1).

Bring the bight up, inverting the lower pair of half knots in the process; and, having also inverted the upper pair of half knots, tuck the bight up through the centre of them (2).

Similarly, tuck both loose ends down through the centre of the lower pair of half knots, exactly as shown (3). The tying is now completed.

ORIGIN

Lydia Chen, in her book *Chinese Knotting* (1981), calls this by its alternative name of plafond knot, after the highly decorated ceilings (or *plafonds*) of Chinese temples, where the knot pattern appears repeatedly as an ornamental motif.

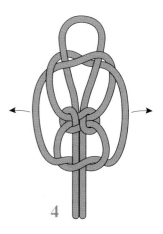

First, tighten the four-part crown that is the centrepiece of this knot, then close up the remaining upper and lower half knots (4).

4

5

6

Lastly, eliminate each side loop by painstakingly working the unwanted slack through the knot until it emerges at one or other of the loose ends, taking care to impart equal tension to every knot part (5, 6).

MOORING HITCH

This alternative to the clove hitch (*see pages 25 and 26*) is quickly tied in the bight and slipped over a vertical mooring post. It may be used to secure a dinghy or even a compliant animal, provided that both are kept under observation.

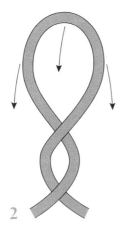

Make a bight in the line and twist it in order to create a couple of elbows (1, 2).

Bend the upper loop down in front, as shown (3).

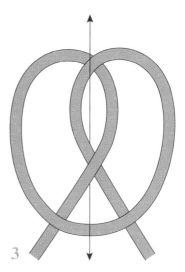

ORIGIN

This tying method was proposed and published as recently as December 2001 by knot craftsman Brian Jarrett of Kent, although the hitch itself is much older.

Then simply slide the resulting layout over the mooring post, as illustrated (4, 5) and tighten the knot.

4

5

TURK'S HEAD
3L x 4B

A Turk's head is a braided bracelet of a knot. The number of different Turk's heads is virtually infinite, but this basic specimen, with its three interwoven parts (leads, L) and four overlapping rim parts (bights, B), is a popular specimen with a variety of uses. It can seize or whip the cut end of a rope to prevent it fraying, or embellish items as diverse as table lamps and flower pots. Tied in gold or silver wire, it makes an unusual finger ring; it is also the sliding neckerchief ring known to young Scouts as a 'woggle'.

Take a turn with the working end round the foundation, cross the end diagonally over the standing part, then take it round once more (1).

From right to left, tuck over one, under one (2).

Lift the right-hand knot part across the left-hand one and then tuck the working end – from left to right – over one, under one (3).

ORIGIN

The Turk's head family is the most diverse of the decorative knot dynasties, the ramifications of which are single-mindedly pursued by some knot tyers, and entire publications have been written about it. Like most knot lore, the tale of its origin is apocryphal.

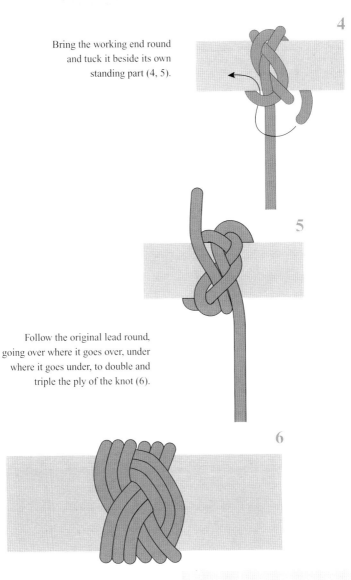

4

Bring the working end round and tuck it beside its own standing part (4, 5).

5

Follow the original lead round, going over where it goes over, under where it goes under, to double and triple the ply of the knot (6).

6

It is said that the Turk's head got its name because the basic knot resembles a turban, and the sailormen of yore called anyone east of Suez who wore this form of headgear (whether Muslim, Hindu or Sikh) 'a Turk'. However, the knot is probably Spanish, and was spread by means of trade and conquest.

TURK'S HEAD
4L x 3B

Every Turk's head knot is identified by two dimensions: first, the number of braided 'leads' (pronounced 'leeds') that determine its width; second, by the number of rim parts, or bights, that make up its circumference. Use this four-lead by three-bight (4L x 3B) Turk's head knot when the 3L x 4B version (*see pages 86–87*) is too narrow for the purpose in hand.

1

Tie a right-handed half knot (one in which the two knot parts spiral to the right) round the rope, rod or other cylindrical foundation (1).

2

Bring the working end round and tuck up – from left to right – under one, over one. Then tuck down – from right to left – over one, under one (2).

3

Bring the working end round to the front once more and make a locking tuck up – from left to right – over one, under one, over one (3).

4

Finally bring the working end down and round to be inserted, under, over, alongside its own standing part (4). By following the original lead with the working end, the knot can be converted into two- or three-ply (5).

5

TURK'S HEAD
3L x 5B

Some members of the Turk's head family not only serve as bracelets, but also look good when tied flat. This one makes a neat tablemat or coaster, an appliqué picture in a frame and – in rope – can serve as a tough clump mat to protect the woodwork or fibreglass of a smart sailboat from dents and scars caused by blocks and other items of rigging hardware.

Make the outline of a pretzel (but unknotted), then tuck the working end as shown, going over one, under one, over one (1).

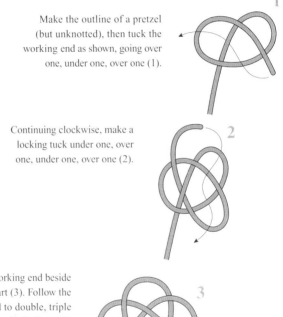

Continuing clockwise, make a locking tuck under one, over one, under one, over one (2).

Lastly, insert the working end beside its own standing part (3). Follow the initial lead round to double, triple or quadruple the knot (4).

TURK'S HEAD
5L x 4B

Any Turk's head knot that has a number of leads and
bights which differ by only one is known as a 'square'
Turk's head; and this one is a versatile knot, being
equally suitable for use as a mundane whipping on a
rope's end (to prevent it fraying) or for some more
ornamental purpose.

1

Take the working end over and round
the foundation, then bring it forwards
again to cross – right to left – over
one (1).

2

Pass it round the back and then go – left
to right – under one and over one (2).

3

Continue tucking the working
end – right to left – over one,
under one, over one (3).

ORIGIN

Although sailors tied various forms
of the Turk's head, South American
vaqueros and Western cowboys executed
even more elaborate ones in braided
rawhide leather horse tack; there is also
evidence of the knot in the tombs of
ancient Egyptian pharaohs.

4

Take the end down, round and back to the front of the work, to make a penultimate locking tuck – left to right once more – under, over, under, over (4).

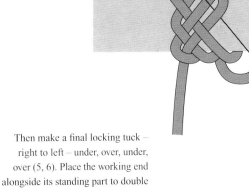

5

Then make a final locking tuck – right to left – under, over, under, over (5, 6). Place the working end alongside its standing part to double or triple the ply of this knot.

6

OVAL MAT

Made in ornamental cord, pairs of this knot could make epaulettes for the uniforms of marching bands. Tied in rope, it becomes a doormat. It may be tied directly onto a flat surface, by hand, with no artificial aids; but early efforts to do so can be made easier by pinning it onto a thick cork or polystyrene ceiling tile or similar baseboard.

Form a trio of overhand loops and interlace them exactly as shown (1).

Tuck the working end – left to right – over one, under one, over two, under one, over one (2).

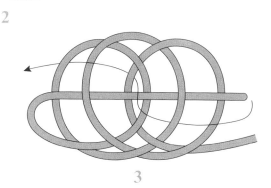

Bring the same end back – right to left – tucking over one, under one, over two (crossing over itself at this point), under one, over one, under one (3).

4

Return – left to right – with a locking
tuck going over, under, over, under,
over, under, over, under, over (4).

5

Bring the working end round to lie beside
its standing part and, following the initial
lead, double the ply of this knot (5, 6).

6

OCEAN BRAID MAT

This wholly symmetrical mat is simpler to tie than the oval mat (*see pages 92–93*) and may be achieved without using pins and board.

Start with the layout shown, and take the working end round anticlockwise, tucking over one, under two, over one, under one, over one, under one (1).

Then make a final locking tuck, over, under, over, under, over (2).

Bring the working end and the standing part together, parallel (3). Double or triple the mat, as desired (4).

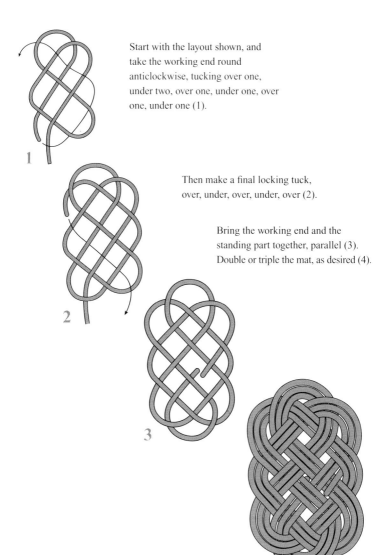

ESKIMO BOWLINE

This bowline is less likely to come apart, if shaken or tugged spasmodically, than its European counterpart, and has a slick trip-&-tighten tying method. In the 20th century it was known to merchant seamen as a Panama bowline, apparently from its use in the lines of ships taken through the canal of that name.

Make an uncompleted overhand knot (1).

Tuck the working end up through it, in a locking tuck that goes over, under, over (2).

Pull on – or load – the standing part, and the initial layout capsizes into the final knot form (3).

Further tightening removes the familiar bowline or sheet bend appearance to create a compact three-part crown (4).

ORIGIN
There is evidence that this unorthodox but handy variant of the common bowline (*see page 30*) was used by a tribe of Arctic Inuits to start rawhide lashings towards the end of the 18th century.

ICHABOD KNOT

A sliding loop or noose like this was employed once upon a time to snare animals and birds for food. It will also start a package lashing, or act as a hitch to rail, ring, spar or post. Pass the standing end through the loop and a running Ichabod knot results, which (like the running bowline, *see page 33*) falls loose when the load is removed.

Form a bight in the end of the line and take the working end round the standing part to create a loop (1).

Now pass the working end twice round both loop legs (2, 3).

ORIGIN

This sliding loop knot was reportedly tied as a hangman's noose at the old Newcastle jail, in the American state of Delaware, in the early half of the 20th century, but was probably used more prosaically by local farmers to tether livestock.

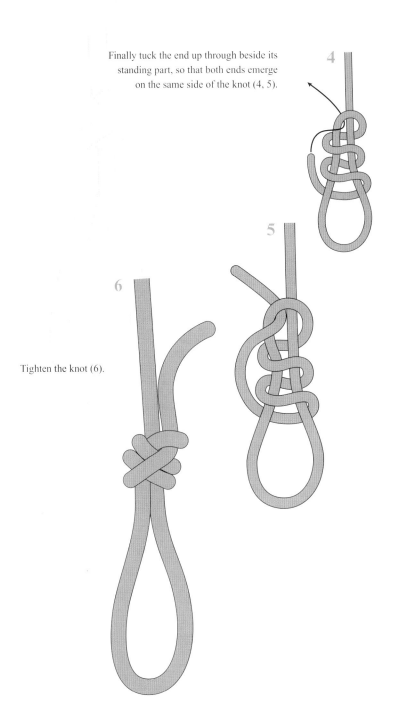

Finally tuck the end up through beside its standing part, so that both ends emerge on the same side of the knot (4, 5).

Tighten the knot (6).

GIBBET KNOT

This alternative to the Ichabod knot (*see pages 96–97*) can be used in exactly the same way; but, given the immense variety of modern cordage, one knot may work better than the other in some materials. Such sliding loops are useful as reusable hitches, to start lashings, and for packages.

Make a bight in the end of the line and then take the working end round the standing part, as shown, to form a loop (1).

Wrap the end three times round both loop legs (2, 3).

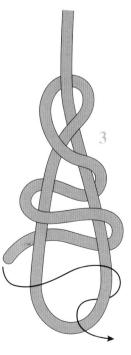

ORIGIN

A gibbet was a gallows from which executed criminals were suspended, so the name of this knot implies that – like the Ichabod knot (*see pages 96–97*) – it too was once a hangman's noose.

Pass the end through the loop, before
tucking it up beside the standing part
so that both ends emerge on the same
side of the knot (4, 5).

Tighten the knot (6).

SANSOME BEND

Knots are like tools: bodgers use and misuse (or abuse) the same few for every task that comes to hand. Craftspeople take the time and trouble to acquire a lot, so as always to have available precisely what is required for the best result. This forgotten knot is worth a try when conventional bends prove unreliable in slick, stretchy or troublesome stuff. It is a tenacious bend and can even remain tight when it is tied in modern bungee cords (shock elastics).

1

Make a bight in one line and tuck the other working end through to wrap twice round the inert end of the bight (1, 2).

2

3

ORIGIN

Englishman Malcolm Hughes learnt this knot from his grandfather, Philip Sansome, who claimed to have used it for joining lengths of elastic when he was a young man in the weaving trade at Loughborough, in Leicester, around 1845.

Pass the working end round both bight legs and then tuck it back, through its own two wrapping turns, to emerge on the opposite side of the knot from its own standing part (3, 4).

4

5

Then tighten the knot (5).

The evolution of knots reveals a mean streak:
once a layout that works manifests itself, it
recurs. See how similar the Bugaboo bend is –
a knot found by Canadian climber Robert
Chisnall, tied in a discarded sling, during
an expedition to the Bugaboo Mountains
in the summer of 1982.

Bugaboo bend

SHEEPSHANK SECURED

One particular use for a sheepshank (other than as a shortening) is to bridge and temporarily safeguard a weak or damaged portion of rope by placing the strain on the other two legs; in this case it is vital that both ends of the knot are secure. There are numerous ways to achieve this, three of which are described here.

weak spot

Method 1: double the retaining loop at each end, to form a clove hitch (1, 2).

Method 2: form an uncompleted overhand knot, as shown, and insert a locking tuck – under, over, under – by pulling the loop through it (1, 2).

Method 3: tie a double overhand knot with the working end round the loop (1, 2).

Caution: use this last version only when the load is light or virtually non-existent, and the stuff in which it is tied has plenty of friction. Because, while it is the neatest and apparently the most secure of the three methods, a heavy pull on both ends will undo this knot.

GROUND LINE HITCH

This secure alternative to the clove hitch (*see pages 25 and 26*) has been used afloat on nets to trawl the seas of the world for cod, and ashore as a picket-line hitch by cavalry. It is a versatile knot that can be employed whenever a line must be attached to an anchorage point to withstand a right-angled load.

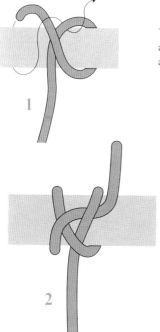

Take a turn round the rail, ring or spar, and lay the working end diagonally across the standing part of the line (1).

Pass the end down round the back and bring it up at the front once more, tucking – left to right – over one, under one (2).

Alternatively, do not pull the end through completely, but leave the draw-loop protruding for quick release (3).

Small and flexible articles attached by means of a single loop to a ring (for example, key fobs or zipper tags) can be lost if excessive wear due to friction causes them to break. Adding an extra couple of knot parts reduces the load on each by one-third. There are two ways in which to achieve this.

Method 1: tuck the fob or tag up through the ring and then down behind itself, in effect tying a half hitch in the doubled line (1, 2).

Method 2: tuck the fob or tag through its own loop, and then arrange the result as shown (1, 2).

ORIGIN

The peerless American knotting author and illustrator Clifford Warren Ashley became interested in the problem of reinforcing ring hitches when a watch guard that he prized began to show signs of wear. He published these two tying methods in 1944.

IMPROVISED HACKAMORE KNOT

Knotted rope halters tied over and round the heads of horses as *ad hoc* bridles to tether, lead, train and ride them have as their basis one of several hackamore knots. These customarily have twin loops emerging from one end of the knot, with a single loop and two long ends at the other end. This version is easier to tie than traditional models.

Fold the rope into three parts, as if to begin a sheepshank (*see pages 23, 24*). Wrap one end round to enclose both legs of the adjacent bight and its own standing part (1, 2).

Wrap the end a second time round all three standing parts, then pull a drawloop through beneath the turns to complete a slipped double overhand knot (3).

ORIGIN

Makeshift headstalls, bridles or harnesses tied in rope have been around for as long as humankind has been catching, breaking and riding horses. This is just one of many such age-old cordage contrivances.

Adjust the resulting loops and
ends to the required length,
then tighten the knot (4).

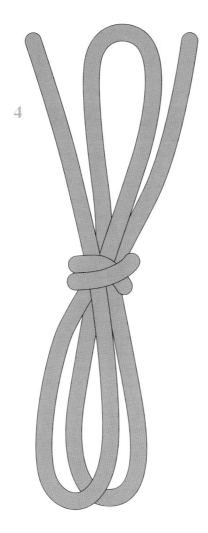

4

FIADOR KNOT

Tying this knot (pronounced 'fee-ah-door') may not go right every time; so if at first you don't succeed, tie, tie and tie again. It forms the basis for a horse's bridle or headstall. Only the knot is described here, its application to the horse's head – with brow-band, ear loops and cheek straps, plus attachments for bit and reins – being a matter for separate tuition from an experienced instructor.

Double a length of rope or cord, double it again and temporarily seize the resulting four parts together with adhesive drafting tape or twine (1, 2).

Bend the single upper loop down, and similarly seize it to the two loose ends (3).

Lift up the single loop and tuck the two loose ends down through it, exactly as shown (4).

ORIGIN

This classic knot is of Spanish origin, but following Theodore Roosevelt's success as commander of a volunteer force of 'rough riders' in the Spanish-American War of 1898, the name was deliberately changed by western US horsemen to the Theodore knot – a term still used today.

Now turn the work round, then tuck each
end in turn up through its respective loop
(5, 6). The tying is now completed.

5

Carefully, so as not to disturb the
positions of the various knotted
parts, remove each tape (the upper
one first), and painstakingly coax
the knot into its final form (7)
before tightening it.

6

7

HORSE DEALER'S HITCH

Tethering a horse is rarely as simple as it appears when Hollywood cowboys dismount outside the saloon or general store and, after a single twirl of reins round a crude wooden hitching rail, leave their mounts unattended. A knot that can be deftly tied in rope or rein, and which a perverse animal cannot easily undo with its teeth, is usually required. This one comes recommended.

1

Pass the end of the halter rope through the ring, at the same time twisting an overhand loop into the standing part (1).

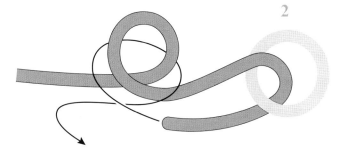

2

Bring the end of the rope back and take it clockwise round the initial loop (2).

ORIGIN

North of England knot tyer A. P. Bloomer was taught this knot in the first half of the 20th century by a horse dealer. Since then, he claims, he has tied it in the dark, in the wet, sometimes with an argumentative horse on the other end, and has never known it to slip.

Then tuck a bight beneath the standing part of the rope and up through the original loop from back to front (3, 4).

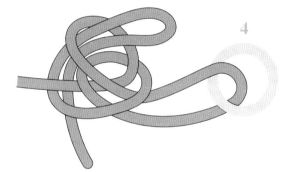

Tighten the knot (5). To undo it, simply tug on the end to pull out the drawloop.

ARMS-AKIMBO LANYARD KNOT

Single-strand lanyard knots like this one can be tied in the finest of threads or thick cord, but something in between – which shows the knot's distinctive outline and texture – is ideal. This knot was once recommended for the cord that secured a gentleman's monocle to the lapel of his jacket, and today would do just as well to suspend reading spectacles round the neck. You can also make a series of these knots into a bracelet, anklet or necklace.

1

Make an overhand loop in cord and pull a bight through it (1, 2).

2

With the working end, form an underhand loop, then lead the end up through the bight – from back to front – and down again to tuck through its own loop (3, 4).

3

ORIGIN

The name derives from the knot's resemblance to a person standing, hands on hips and elbows stuck out sideways.

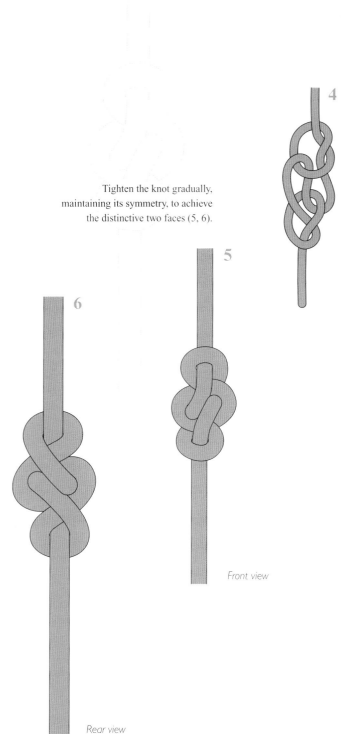

Tighten the knot gradually, maintaining its symmetry, to achieve the distinctive two faces (5, 6).

4

5

Front view

6

Rear view

CHINESE CLOVERLEAF KNOT

Like the preceding lanyard knot (*see pages 112–113*), this is purely decorative, but is intriguing to tie for its own sake.

Make a bight in the cord, then bring the end round to tuck a second bight – over, under – through the first one (1).

Repeat the process (2).

Then, continuing clockwise, take the working end and insert a locking tuck (inwards) over, under, over, over, to return (outwards) under, under, under, over. The resulting layout tightens into a triangular knot form, with three optional loops, for a neck lanyard (3).

ORIGIN

This is one of the simpler knots from a family of increasingly elaborate Chinese ornamental knots, used to adorn clothing or attach amulets and other valued items. Generations of Chinese children, in common with their Western counterparts, have been told the clover is a lucky plant.

Otherwise, before tightening the knot, tuck the working end up through the centre of the knot, as shown (4).

4

Then tighten carefully to create a handsome square-shaped and solid knot (5).

5

MYSTIC KNOT

This knot, which has Buddhist connotations and is also known as the Pan Chang knot, makes an eye-catching loop in the end of any neck lanyard. It is easier to tie if each stage is pinned onto a cork or polystyrene tile or board, rather than attempted directly by hand on a flat surface, although this is not essential.

1

Arrange the first two interlaced layers, as shown, with one working end (1).

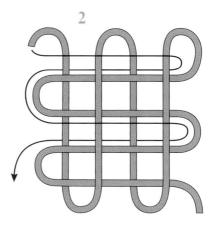

2

Then, with the other end, create reciprocal bights (2, 3).

ORIGIN

According to the Chinese knotting writer Lydia Chen, the mystic or Pan Chang knot is one of the eight Buddhist Treasures, its convolutions being a tangible reminder of the cyclical nature of all existence, which is one of the basic precepts in Chinese Buddhism.

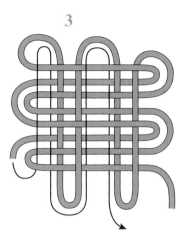

3

During tightening, which must be done cautiously so as not to distort the slack knot, the seemingly two-dimensional layout separates into an upper and lower layer, forming the two faces of the finished knot (4).

4

The primary bottom loop is indispensable, if the knot is part of a lanyard, but the six secondary lateral loops may be left open or tightened.

BLIMP KNOT

After the preceding two knots, this one is easy. It is another simple embellishment for a lanyard, which resembles the zeppelin bend (*see pages 66–67*), but is smaller and softer, hence its whimsical name (a 'blimp' being a light, non-rigid, often tethered aircraft or large balloon).

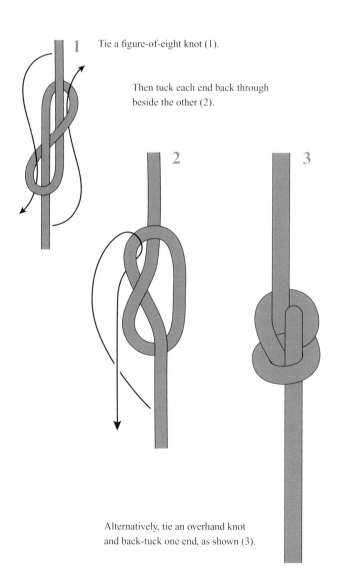

Tie a figure-of-eight knot (1).

Then tuck each end back through beside the other (2).

Alternatively, tie an overhand knot and back-tuck one end, as shown (3).

Innovative knots

INNOVATIVE KNOTS

'Given a piece of string, man will find some new way of tying a knot with it.'

CAPTAIN PAUL HARRISON, 1964

New knots are being devised or discovered all the time, but to be assured of a welcome, any newcomer needs to be in some way superior to those knots already in use. The knots in this section have all surfaced within the past couple of decades – or, perhaps, reappeared after a period of neglect – but it may be another 20 years before any one of them becomes an established favourite.

INTRODUCTION

The legacy bequeathed to us by the ancients and by old-time sailormen, according to the prolific knotting writer Geoffrey Budworth, is certainly not all there is to know about knotting. New knots are invented or encountered every year, while old and neglected ones (perhaps viewed with disfavour by previous generations, for whom they behaved poorly in the cordage then available) are resurrected, rehabilitated and found to work reliably in modern synthetic materials.

There are knotting devotees who argue that knots cannot be 'invented', but – like scientific laws – can only be discovered. A more realistic assessment is perhaps that by John Smith of Surrey, who (writing in *Knotting Matters,* in July 1989) pointed out that some knots undoubtedly result from knowledge and skill purposefully applied to achieve a specific outcome. Such knots are surely invented (or at least developed) by the individuals who create them. Other knots come about by accident, through fiddling fingers and curious minds. Thirdly, there is the 'Aha!' experience, when some serendipitous combination of turns and tucks, in suitable cordage, is perceived by an alert individual to be an innovative piece of knotting. Smith summed up his three-sided hypothesis as Invention, Accident or Observation.

Innovative knots must ultimately be assessed by criteria that define fitness of purpose, just as for traditional knots, namely: a form readily learnt and taught; ease of tying and untying; adequate strength and security; one or more desirable qualities; and a broad range of applications. The knotting writer and researcher Pieter van de Griend summarizes all of this as 'Survival of the Simplest', although the term 'simple' may seem an understatement when learning (say) one of the 'exploding' knots by Peter Suber included in this section, or Olivier Peron's corkscrew knot.

Exploding clove hitch

MILLER'S KNOT

Binding knots for the necks of sacks need to be quickly
applied, be secure without jamming and be just as easily
untied. When binding a hard and unyielding item (such as
a hosepipe on a tap), use soft and stretchy cord for the best
effect; on a soft foundation (such as a sack), use hard stuff
that will bite into it.

Take the working end twice round the sack's
neck and bring the standing part diagonally
across the other inert part (1, 2).

1

Tuck the working end as shown (3).

2

Pull on both ends to
tighten the knot (4).

3

ORIGIN
The miller's knot dates back to the days
of windmills, when grain and seed
(measured in archaic bushels and pecks)
were ground for staple foods such as
bread and cattle feed, and were then
bagged up by the miller into sacks.

4

Bracelet binding

For those occasions when some ornamentation is desirable, the extra effort taken to tie this knot (also known as the sack knot) is repaid by the neat four-part diamond crown that results.

Wrap the working end twice round the object, then tuck it beneath the two inert turns and beneath itself in the form of a half hitch (1, 2).

1

2

Tuck the other end in the same manner (3), then work the knot snug and tight (4).

3

4

ORIGIN
Sack knots of several different sorts, like this one, were used in previous centuries, when various granular or powdered dry goods were simply bagged in flax, jute or hessian sacks.

JULIE'S HITCH

This hitch has proved to be handy when an anchorage point (such as an overhead rail or a trailer axle) is beyond comfortable reach, in which case the doubled end of a line may be thrown or otherwise passed round it. However, the actual knot has to be tied closer to hand.

Double the end of the line and loop, and pass the resulting bight over the distant anchorage point. Take the working end round the standing part and tuck it through the bight, from front to back (1, 2).

Tuck the working end through the bight a second time (3), and lead it down beside the standing part (4).

ORIGIN

The knot is named after Geoffrey Budworth's younger daughter Julie, who discovered it for herself in 1974 when she was just nine years old. It was included in his *Knot Book* in 1983.

Carefully tighten the knot, so that the twin loops compensate for an uneven load by feeding one into the other (5).

5

It is advisable to secure the working end to the standing part by means of a bowline or other back-up knot (6).

6

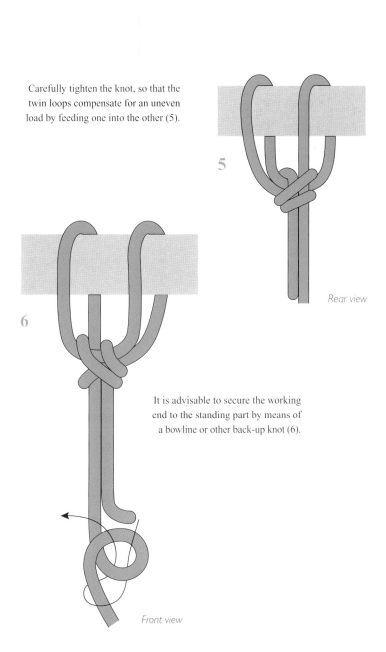

Rear view

Front view

FRUSTRATOR

This binding is kin to the constrictor knot (*see pages 47–51*). Not only is it secure in use, but it also resists attempts to undo it (hence its name). It works best when tied in the bight, although it is not impossible to make this knot with an end.

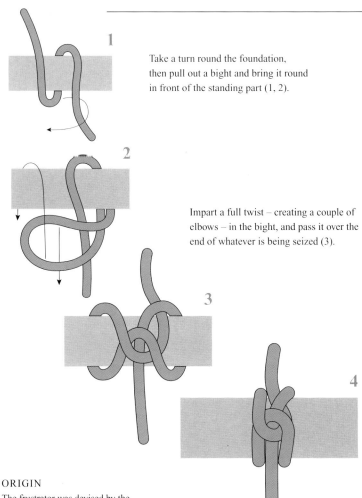

1

Take a turn round the foundation, then pull out a bight and bring it round in front of the standing part (1, 2).

2

Impart a full twist – creating a couple of elbows – in the bight, and pass it over the end of whatever is being seized (3).

3

4

ORIGIN

The frustrator was devised by the late research scientist and inventor Dr Harry Asher. It first appeared in *A New System of Knotting – Volume II*, written by him and published in 1986 by the International Guild of Knot Tying.

Pull on both ends to tighten the knot (4). Once it jams, the ends may be cut short.

RING HITCH DOUBLED

You can use this hitch to join two rings, eyes or swivels by means of a continuous sling or strop. Despite the fact that it looks difficult to accomplish, it is actually quite easy to tie and may be done in a variety of stuff, ranging from webbing to cord and tape, on any scale.

Take the end of the sling through one of the rings, then pass it through itself, thereby creating a simple ring hitch (1).

Next, pass the remaining bight through the second ring, beneath the crossing loop, and completely over the first ring (2).

Tighten the working bight behind the initial ring hitch to interlock the various parts of the knot (3, 4).

ORIGIN

This hitch may date back to medieval times, although it was recently rediscovered by Joe McNicholas of Pennsylvania.

Clinging Clara hitch

This hitch was designed to withstand a longitudinal pull upon a cord that is attached to a hawser-laid rope. It has two distinct forms.

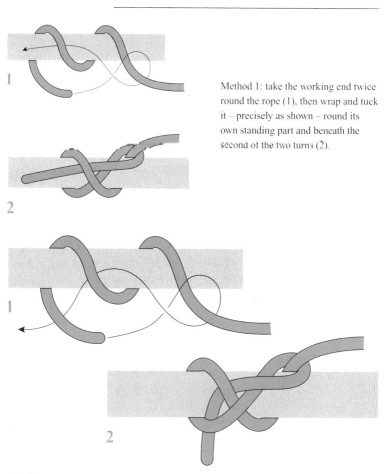

Method 1: take the working end twice round the rope (1), then wrap and tuck it – precisely as shown – round its own standing part and beneath the second of the two turns (2).

ORIGIN

This hitch (and the two derivatives that follow) is another innovative knot, first published in 1986, from the active mind and fingers of the late Dr Harry Asher.

Method 2: start as if tying method 1, but finally tuck the working end beneath two knot parts, rather than one (1, 2).

This superior version of the clinging Clara hitch (*see opposite*) appears to be able to withstand greater strains on its inherent strength and security; but, like all innovative knots, only continual use over time will reveal whether or not it deserves its title.

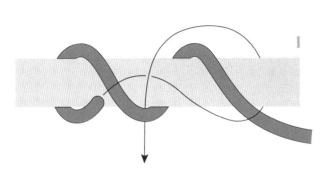

Wrap the working end twice round the hawser, and then bring it back beyond its own standing part and round the rope once more, but in the opposite direction (1).

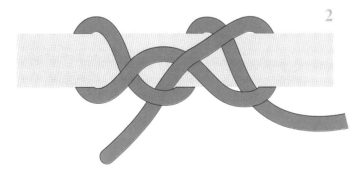

Tuck the working end – over two, under one – as shown (2).

Dr Harry Asher concocted this hitch to withstand a longitudinal pull on a smooth spar and successfully demonstrated it in 1986, on the display stand of the International Guild of Knot Tyers at the annual Boat Show, held in Earls Court exhibition hall, when it coped with a pull towards the narrow end of a billiard cue.

1

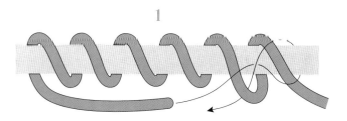

Lead the working end at least six turns round the foundation, then bring it back beyond its own standing part and round the rope once more, but in the opposite direction (1).

2

Tuck the working end – over two, under one – as shown (2), as for the Queen Clara hitch (*see page 129*).

LIFTING HITCH

Hoisting scaffold poles, a boat mast or other smooth, heavy lengths requires a hitch with friction to withstand a sustained longitudinal pull, yet it ought to be readily applied and just as easily cast off again. This hitch is one of many with those very qualities.

Wrap the working end tightly, in a downwards direction, six to eight times round the object to be lifted (1).

Then bring the end up and round the standing part (2).

Lastly, take it down once more, and apply a restraining half hitch (3).

ORIGIN

This lifting hitch is similar to those featured in his excellent *A Fresh Approach to Knotting and Ropework* by Charles Warner, published in 1992.

PEACE KNOT

This unusual fixed-loop knot replaces the bowline and other such knots, if these are likely to jam and become hard to untie, with the useful property that it falls apart (no further untying required) when the drawloop is removed.

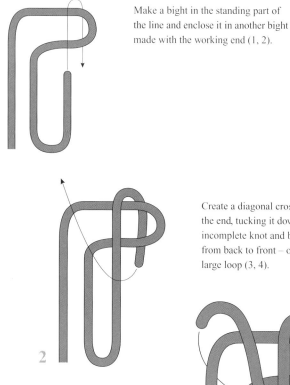

Make a bight in the standing part of the line and enclose it in another bight made with the working end (1, 2).

Create a diagonal crossing with the end, tucking it down behind the incomplete knot and bringing it – from back to front – out through the large loop (3, 4).

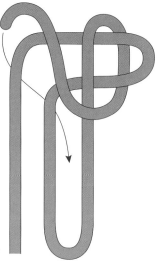

ORIGIN

The Faroese knotting writer/researcher Pieter van de Griend thought up this knot while working on the waterfront at Terneuzen, and published it in 1986. He and other seamen used it, tied in 20-mm(⅞-inch) diameter nylon rope, to hoist mooring lines from ship to jetty.

Finally, tuck a drawloop up through the initial bight (5) and tighten the knot (6).

Although not especially strong, the peace knot was secure enough to do the job without spilling, and was more easily untied than bowlines, which jammed when heavily loaded (or so the longshoremen forcibly complained).

BUBBLE KNOT

The odd name gives no clue to the use of this knot, which is as a kind of button-&-loop fastening that may be applied and cast off easily in many varied situations.

In a short length of cord tie a figure-of-eight knot, then take one end up through and round the knot to tuck as shown (1).

Introduce the rope that the fastening will serve, tucking and tying as illustrated (2, 3).

ORIGIN

This knot appeared in issue no. 403 (July 2000) of the British monthly magazine *Practical Boat Owner*, and subsequently in issue no. 74 (March 2002) of *Knotting Matters*.

Lastly, add a figure-of-eight knot (or an Ashley's stopper knot) to the cord end that lies alongside the loop and tighten the entire contrivance (4).

Feed the loop through the hole in the sheet or other material, insert the knotted end, and tighten again (5).

It was dreamt up by Michael Collis, who used it as a quick and easy means of swapping the leads or sheets from one jib sail to another. He reported that the knot had never shaken loose (not even in a force six across the North Sea).

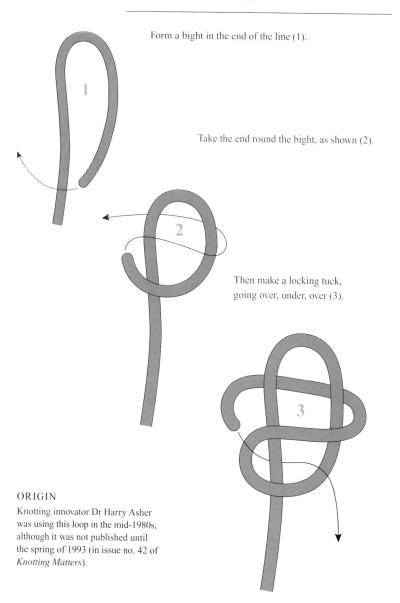

LOCKING LOOP

This knot is one of several slide-&-grip knots that can be shifted by hand to adjust the size of the loop, but which (when loaded) locks firmly into place by creating an abrupt bend in the standing part of the line.

Form a bight in the end of the line (1).

Take the end round the bight, as shown (2).

Then make a locking tuck, going over, under, over (3).

ORIGIN

Knotting innovator Dr Harry Asher was using this loop in the mid-1980s, although it was not published until the spring of 1993 (in issue no. 42 of *Knotting Matters*).

Tighten the knot just enough to secure it,
while still letting it shift as required (4).

Add a drawloop, tucking the working
end back alongside itself. This knot has
two distinct faces that reveal the
mechanism by which it works (5, 6).

Front view

Rear view

SLIP-&-NIP NOOSE

This noose not only makes a quick fastening to a rail, post or spar, but (if tightened) also withstands a longitudinal pull (without the usual numerous wrapping turns that are characteristic of such hitches). It incorporates a useful pinching mechanism, whereby pushing the two enclosing bights closer together tightens the knot, but separating them makes it easier to untie.

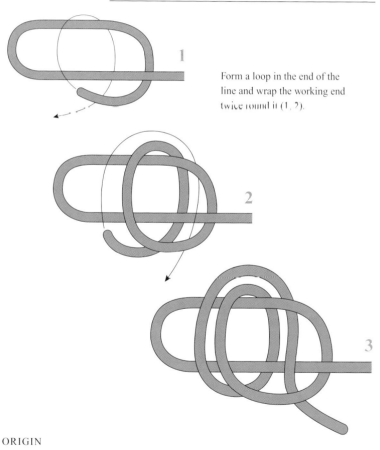

Form a loop in the end of the line and wrap the working end twice round it (1, 2).

ORIGIN

Dr Brooks A. Mick, MD, of Findlay, Ohio, published this loop knot in issue no. 8 (summer 1984) of *Knotting Matters*.

Tuck the end down between the standing part of the line and the initial turn (3).

Tighten the knot (4), and push the
two enclosing loops together (5).

THE INNOMIKNOT

This versatile, general-purpose, heavy-duty hitch can be tied in the bight. From tethering an animal to overcoming a wilderness challenge, its applications are many.

1

Pass the end of the line round the post or other anchorage point, make a loop and further twist it to form a couple of elbows (1, 2, 3).

2

3

ORIGIN

Dr Les F. Osborne, MD, of Vashon Island in Washington State, sent this loop knot to the National Maritime Museum at Greenwich, England, in the early 1980s. It was, he reported, tied easily and quickly in the dark, and was also readily released under tension.

4

Then pick up a bight in the standing part, bring it across in front of the post, and tuck it down through the loop just formed (4, 5).

5

Tighten the knot (6).

6

The knot was designed to tie down aircraft in the southwest Pacific during World War Two, and Osborne initially knew it as the 'No name knot'. As bits of anatomy without a name are said to be 'innominate', Geoffrey Budworth suggested (and Osborne agreed) that it made sense to call this the innomiknot.

EXPLODING CLOVE HITCH

Most so-called 'slipped' knots, which incorporate a quick-release drawloop, nevertheless require some untying after the loop has been freed. Shoelaces are an everyday example. This knot – in common with the five that follow – falls apart (or 'explodes') completely when the drawloop is freed. The Lapp and peace knots (*see pages 76 and 132–133 respectively*) also share this property.

1

Take the working end round the anchorage point, and then make a couple of overhand loops in the standing part of the line (1).

2

Overlap the loops, as shown (2), and pull a bight from the working end through them (3).

3

Then tighten the knot (4). To release, tug on the short end.

4

ORIGIN

This knot was devised by Peter Suber of Richmond, Indiana, and it featured as 'Knot of the Month' in *Boating* magazine in October 1999.

EXPLODING FIGURE-OF-EIGHT HITCH

Like the preceding knot (as well as those that follow), this hitch of Peter Suber's is primarily intended by its innovator for use in climbing and outdoor pursuits; and in this connection there are extra subtleties concerned with tying, tightening and releasing it, not dealt with here. Suber's own far more detailed descriptions and analyses can be found on his Internet website (*see page 205*).

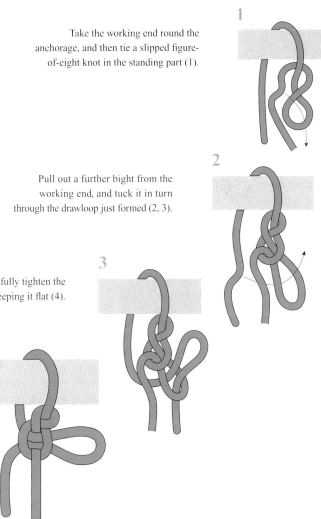

Take the working end round the anchorage, and then tie a slipped figure-of-eight knot in the standing part (1).

Pull out a further bight from the working end, and tuck it in turn through the drawloop just formed (2, 3).

Carefully tighten the knot, keeping it flat (4).

EXPLODING BUTTERFLY HITCH

The figure-of-eight layout that is apparent during the tying of this knot disappears when it is tightened, and it then acquires the useful quality of becoming a slide-&-lock loop.

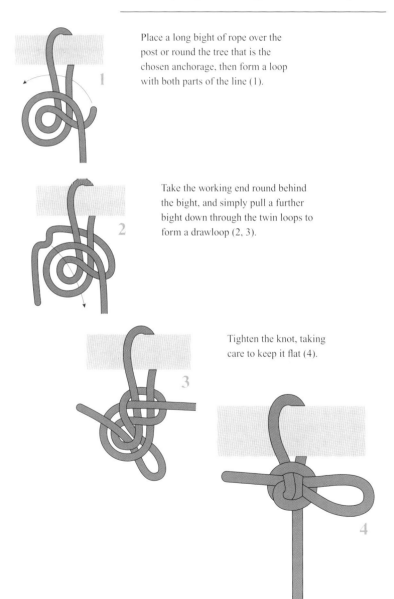

Place a long bight of rope over the post or round the tree that is the chosen anchorage, then form a loop with both parts of the line (1).

Take the working end round behind the bight, and simply pull a further bight down through the twin loops to form a drawloop (2, 3).

Tighten the knot, taking care to keep it flat (4).

Exploding sheet bend

This knot is the favourite (in this series of six 'exploding' knots) of the inventor, Peter Suber. It too is a useful slide-&-lock loop.

Pass the working end round the anchorage and lift up a bight within the standing part (1).

Form an underhand loop with the working end, and fit it in the form of a half hitch over the lower bight in the standing part (2).

Then pull a bight from the end through the bight beneath the half hitch (3). Tighten the knot, taking care to keep it flat (4).

EXPLODING CHINESE CROWN HITCH

Despite its apparent complexity, this knot (devised, like the five other 'exploding' hitches, by Peter Suber) can be tied in seconds.

Pass the working end round the anchorage, pick up a bight in the standing part and tuck the working end through it, as shown (1).

Pass the end round the back of everything, from right to left, and then pull a bight through the original loop (2, 3).

Tighten the whole knot carefully,
keeping it flat (4, 5).

EXPLODING DOUBLE CARRICK HITCH

This is the last of the six super 'exploding' knots invented by Peter Suber, from Richmond, Indiana.

Pass the working end over the anchorage and form an underhand loop in the standing part (1).

Bring the short end, from left to right, beneath the loop and over the standing part (2).

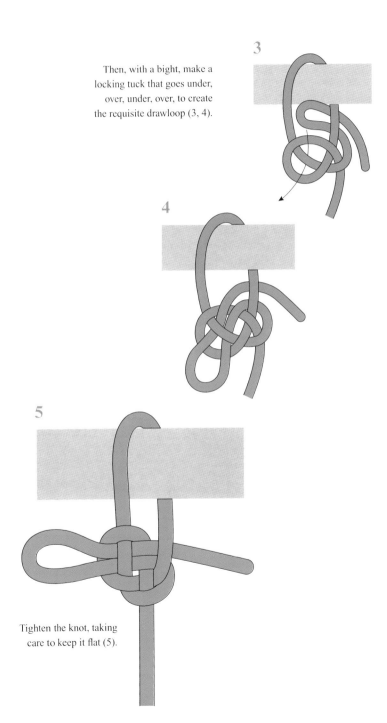

3

Then, with a bight, make a
locking tuck that goes under,
over, under, over, to create
the requisite drawloop (3, 4).

4

5

Tighten the knot, taking
care to keep it flat (5).

CORKSCREW KNOT

It is claimed that this knot is superior to many other climbing knots in rappelling (abseiling) on static or dynamic lines; and that, because it withstands shock loading of various intensities and differing frequencies, it is suited to acrobatic work, tree cutting, et cetera. It can be tied in the bight and released from a distance, limited only by the doubled length of the rope. There are two different methods of tying the corkscrew.

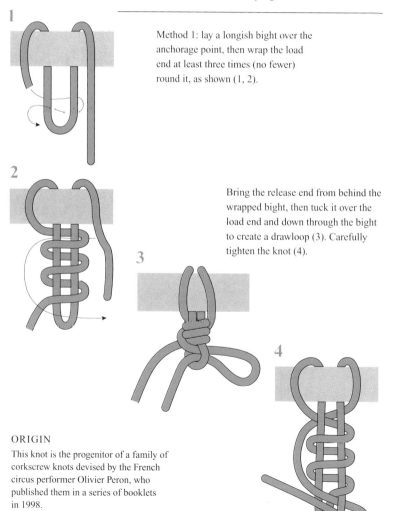

Method 1: lay a longish bight over the anchorage point, then wrap the load end at least three times (no fewer) round it, as shown (1, 2).

Bring the release end from behind the wrapped bight, then tuck it over the load end and down through the bight to create a drawloop (3). Carefully tighten the knot (4).

ORIGIN

This knot is the progenitor of a family of corkscrew knots devised by the French circus performer Olivier Peron, who published them in a series of booklets in 1998.

Method 2: to equalize the load
between a couple of anchorages,
double the rope and arrange it round
both anchorages, as shown (1).

1

Wrap the load end as before, then
take a turn (in the opposite direction)
with the release end, before tucking
to create the required drawloop (2).

2

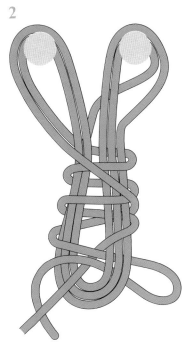

KATHERINE'S KNOT

Essentially a 'left-handed' sheet bend (that is, one in which the short ends emerge on opposite sides of the knot), this compact little bend has been back-tucked to improve its security.

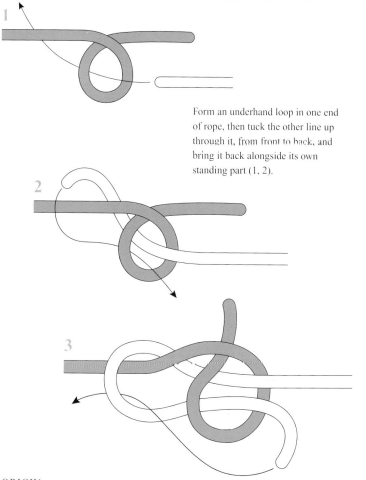

Form an underhand loop in one end of rope, then tuck the other line up through it, from front to back, and bring it back alongside its own standing part (1, 2).

ORIGIN

This knot was discovered – or perhaps merely rediscovered – in 1982 by Katherine M. Saunders, of Halesowen in the West Midlands and was published in issue no. 7 of *Knotting Matters*.

Tuck the working end of the doubled line though its own bight (3, 4).

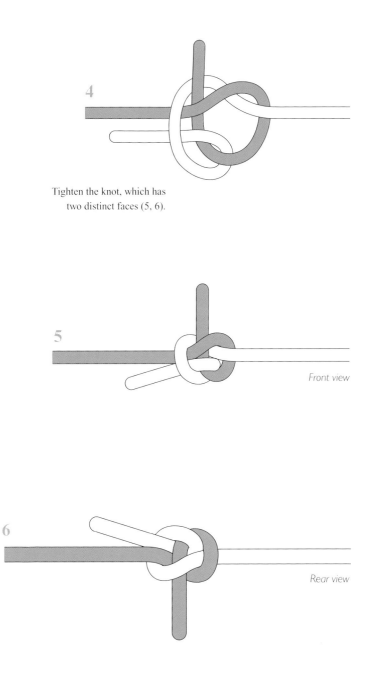

4

Tighten the knot, which has
two distinct faces (5, 6).

5

Front view

6

Rear view

SIMPLE SIMON BEND

You can use this snug and secure bend to join two lines of different thickness when the sheet bend (*see pages 35, 36 and 37*) might prove inadequate.

Make a bight in one line, then tuck the other line up through and round it, as shown (1, 2).

ORIGIN

This is yet another knot (related to the double crossed Simon bend that follows) that first appeared in *A New System of Knotting – Volume I* by Dr Harry Asher, which was published in 1986 by the International Guild of Knot Tyers.

Bring the working end diagonally
across itself, then tuck it one final time,
to emerge from the initial bight on the
same side as its own standing part (3).

Pull on both legs in order to
tighten the knot (4).

DOUBLE CROSSED SIMON BEND

Like the simple Simon bend (*see pages 154–155*), this knot is intended to join two ropes or cords that are of somewhat dissimilar size or construction.

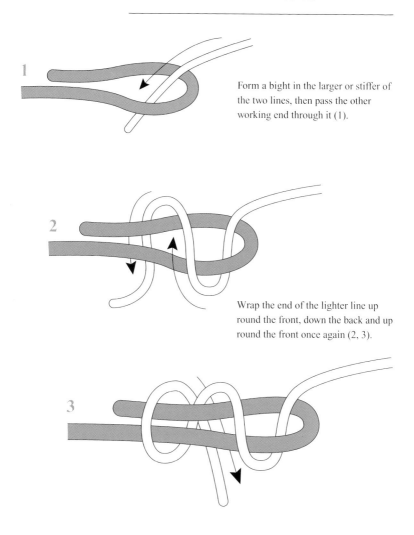

Form a bight in the larger or stiffer of the two lines, then pass the other working end through it (1).

Wrap the end of the lighter line up round the front, down the back and up round the front once again (2, 3).

Now make a return journey, going
over at each crossing point and
finally tucking the working end up
beside its own standing part (4, 5).

Pull on both legs of each line to
tighten the knot (6).

SYMMETRIC HAWSER BEND I

This bend is secure in ropes of similar size and construction, and its comparatively gentle curves make it particularly suitable for larger ropes and cables.

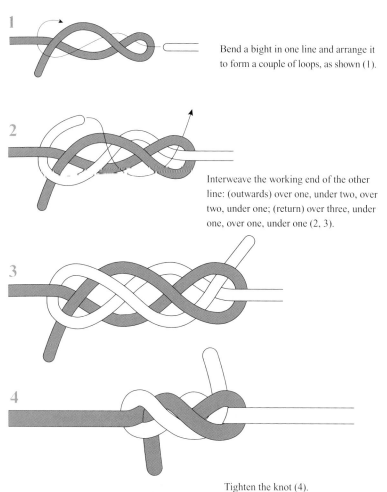

Bend a bight in one line and arrange it to form a couple of loops, as shown (1).

Interweave the working end of the other line: (outwards) over one, under two, over two, under one; (return) over three, under one, over one, under one (2, 3).

Tighten the knot (4).

ORIGIN

Jack Reinmann from Ohio created this secure and good-looking bend (together with the one that follows) and published details of both in issue no. 43 (summer 1993) of *Knotting Matters*.

Symmetric hawser bend II

This alternative may be superior to the preceding knot, and it can be used in lines that differ somewhat in size and construction.

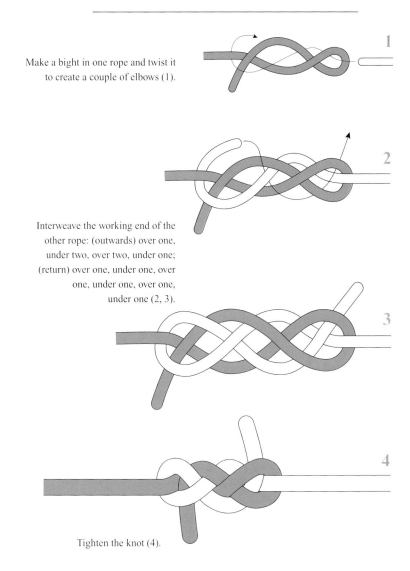

Make a bight in one rope and twist it to create a couple of elbows (1).

Interweave the working end of the other rope: (outwards) over one, under two, over two, under one; (return) over one, under one, over one, under one, over one, under one (2, 3).

Tighten the knot (4).

BROACH BEND

Use this compact interwoven bend for smaller diameters than the preceding hawser bends (*see pages 158–159*). Although it requires careful tightening – otherwise it can slip and pull apart in the early stages – it will then hold in slick or slippery materials that cause lesser bends to fail.

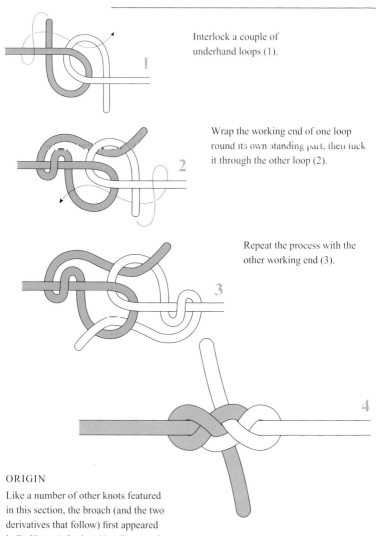

Interlock a couple of underhand loops (1).

Wrap the working end of one loop round its own standing part, then tuck it through the other loop (2).

Repeat the process with the other working end (3).

ORIGIN

Like a number of other knots featured in this section, the broach (and the two derivatives that follow) first appeared in Dr Harry Asher's *A New System of Knotting – Volume I,* published in 1986.

Tighten the knot very carefully (4).

TUCKED BROACH BEND

For added insurance with ultra-smooth materials that
might otherwise do a Houdini and slip free, use this
beefed-up broach bend.

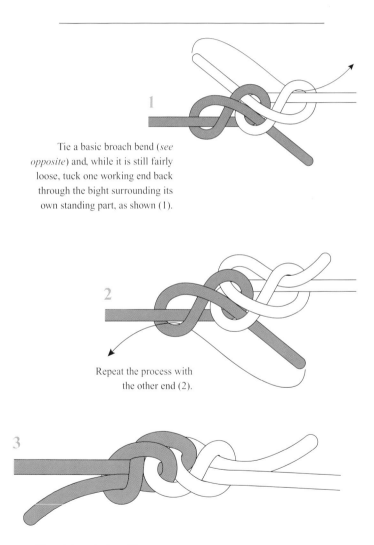

Tie a basic broach bend (*see
opposite*) and, while it is still fairly
loose, tuck one working end back
through the bight surrounding its
own standing part, as shown (1).

Repeat the process with
the other end (2).

Then tighten the knot (3).

BROACH LOOP

Bends can often be made into loops (or, conversely, loops can be made into bends) and the broach loop offers a good example of this.

Lay out an uncompleted figure-of-eight knot in the end of one line (1).

Then, instead of tucking the working end, lead it round and insert it through the lower part, to create the required loop (2).

Wrap and tuck the working end, as shown (3).

Tighten the knot (4).

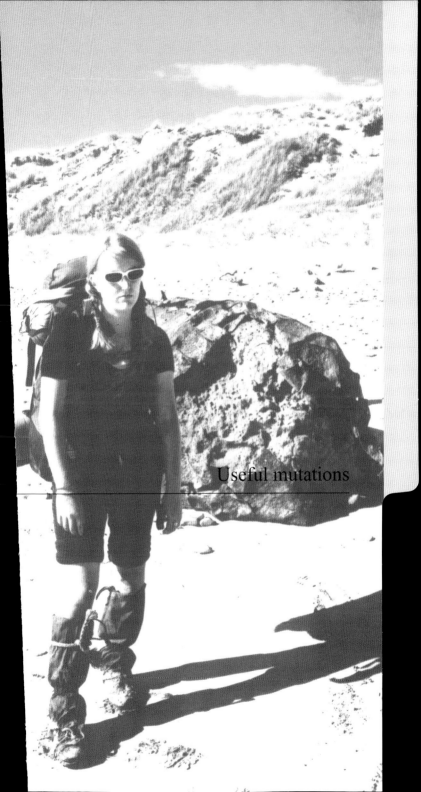

Useful mutations

USEFUL MUTATIONS

'But knotting is merely the application of certain mechanical principles, and a principle itself can hardly become obsolete. As conditions change, new applications are bound to appear.'

CLIFFORD W. ASHLEY, 1944

We may know less than half of all there is to discover about knotting. Not only are new knots still being generated, but long-established ones metamorphose into diverse variants. Far from being a moribund breed, dying from neglect, knots are vibrantly alive and multiplying. Those individuals who have a hand in each new birth or mutation, some of whom are mentioned in this section, add to the useful sum of human knowledge.

INTRODUCTION

Can you tie a Turk's head? This question is frequently asked of knotting practitioners, to which they can only respond, 'Which one?' Because, without wishing to dismiss or put down their questioners, there are hundreds of Turk's head knots of different dimensions and weaves that can easily enough be tied – just five of which are described in this book. Thousands more are theoretically feasible, given enough time, ingenuity and cord.

From the figure-of-eight stopper knot evolve more elaborate loops, bends and hitches. Single loop knots can be adapted to become double, triple or multiple loop knots, a few of which can be applied in peculiar ways (as a jury mast knot, an improvised horse bridle or in the form of a chain stitch lashing).

Different tying methods may lead – either intentionally or by chance – to knot variants, while tying material that differs greatly in its construction may result in the emergence of a knot that suits it (see the collared hitch tied in tape or webbing). Knots that are amenable to being tied in flat tape or webbing, and which have already been mentioned, include: the clove hitch; the pole hitch; the buntline hitch; the ossel hitch; the water knot; the ground line hitch; and some ring hitches.

Knots tied a different way, in uncommon cordage, or used for a different purpose can acquire not only another name but another character. The Piwich knot is an adaptation of what sailors would otherwise call an anchor bend; the sheet bend, when executed in woolen yarns, becomes a weaver's knot. And the classic Prusik knot, first created to mend the broken strings of musical instruments, and subsequently used by climbers, becomes in this section a bottle, jar or jug sling. Mutations are simply a response to altered needs.

Chain stitch lashing

FIGURE-OF-EIGHT LOOP

The advantage of tying a loop in this way – as those who use life-support knots will readily appreciate – is that it may be pulled wide open, from both directions at once, without loss of knot integrity.

Tie a figure-of-eight knot loosely in the standing part of the line (1).

Then insert the working end at the top of the knot, forming a large loop of the required size in the process, and follow the initial lead round until the knot has been duplicated (2, 3, 4).

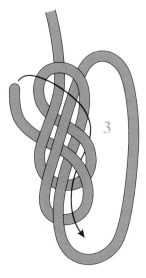

ORIGIN

Dan Lehman of Virginia, a dedicated knot researcher and writer, spotted this knot used as the clip-into loop of top-roping rock climbers, and published it in issue no. 26 of *Knotting Matters* (January 1989).

Tighten the knot methodically and as neatly as possible (5).

167

DOUBLE ANGLER'S LOOP

Twin loops have a number of uses, from improvised chair rescue knots to attachment points for fly-fishing lurers, and this adaptation of the basic angler's loop (*see pages 68–69*) is an ingenious example.

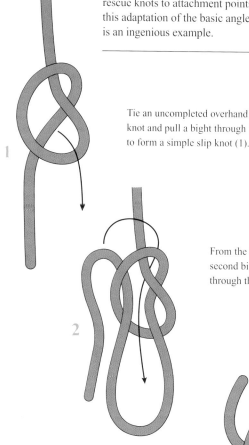

Tie an uncompleted overhand knot and pull a bight through it to form a simple slip knot (1).

From the long working end, lift a second bight and tuck it in turn down through the slip knot just formed (2).

ORIGIN

This knot first appeared in *A Fresh Approach to Knotting and Ropework* by Charles Warner, which was published in 1992.

169

Finally lead the working end across the front of the standing part and tuck it, as shown (3, 4).

4

The two distinctive faces (front and rear) of the basic angler's loop are still just recognizable in this bulkier twin-loop version (5, 6).

5

Rear view

6

Front view

BRUMMYCHAM BOWLINE

This double loop is intended to be used only when both ends of the rope are available for tying it. It can, however, be tied in a way similar to that already described for the bowline in the bight (*see pages 72–73*) and may also be made with more than two turns as loops. Indeed, it is a useful method of coiling and hanging up rope for storage.

1

Begin by coiling the rope and, when two large loops appear, add a small underhand loop in the standing part (1).

Tuck the upper bights of both larger loops up through the small loop (2), then pass all of the standing part of the line through these two bights (3).

2

ORIGIN

The active Dr Harry Asher produced this knot, naming it after his home city of Birmingham. It first appeared in his *A New System of Knotting* (1986) and later in his *The Alternative Knot Book* (1989).

Bed the knot down
neatly and tighten it (4).

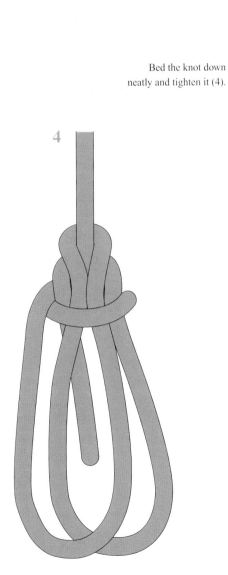

ROBUST HANDCUFF KNOT

This twin-loop knot is an elaboration of the strangle knot *(see page 46)* and, like other so-called 'handcuff' knots, is really no such thing. It is far more likely to be tied as a make-&-mend suitcase handle or gift-package ornamentation, or (in rope) for civil engineering or salvage operations.

Make a bight in one end of a lanyard or lashing and wrap the end round it in a series of not less than three turns (1, 2).

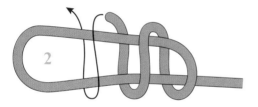

Then tuck a bight from the working end back through the turns, alongside the standing part of the line (3).

ORIGIN

This knot appeared in *The Ashley Book of Knots* (originally published in New York in 1944) by Clifford W. Ashley, who described it at that time as a 'commercial cord curtain holdback'.

Pull the standing leg of both loops in opposite directions to tighten the knot (4).

Adjust the loops to the required size and lock each in turn with a half hitch applied over its opposite number (5, 6).

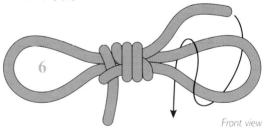

Front view

Tighten the knot again (7).

Rear view

JURY MAST KNOT

Today this knot has become a mere party-piece for knot tyers keen to impress with their skill and dexterity. It can also be used, however, to embellish the uniforms of bandsmen and women, or as a central motif in appliqué pictures and embroidery; or even as an improvised hackamore or rope bridle for horse, mule, camel or other saddled creature.

Form three underhand loops, one after the other, and overlap them as shown (1, 2).

ORIGIN

A 'jury mast' was a temporary or occasional mast on a newly launched ship that did not yet have its permanent masts and spars; it could also serve in the short term in place of a mast that had been carried away in a storm, battle or some other extraordinary event.

Pull the right-hand edge of the left-hand loop to the right, going over, under, over; at the same time, pull the left-hand edge of the right-hand loop to the left, going under, over, under (3).

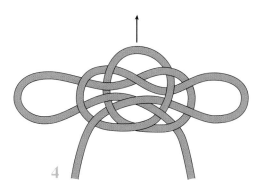

Obtain the necessary slack to pull
out the middle loop (4, 5). Insert
whatever is to be seized, through
the central space marked X.

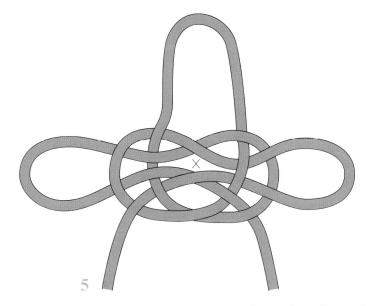

The jury mast knot was a rigger's
expedient – an interwoven bracelet
to whose loops and ends could be
attached the necessary stays in order
to raise and hold such a mast upright.

TURK'S HEAD
2L x 5B

This unassuming relative of the diverse Turk's head family (*see also pages 86–91*) deserves to be better known. Use it in cord or thong as ornamentation for fancy knotting or braided leather work. Tie it round rubish bins and plant pots. Wear it as a bracelet, anklet or finger ring.

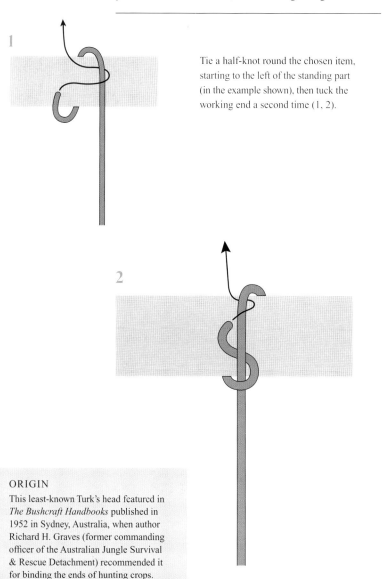

1

Tie a half-knot round the chosen item, starting to the left of the standing part (in the example shown), then tuck the working end a second time (1, 2).

2

ORIGIN

This least-known Turk's head featured in *The Bushcraft Handbooks* published in 1952 in Sydney, Australia, when author Richard H. Graves (former commanding officer of the Australian Jungle Survival & Rescue Detachment) recommended it for binding the ends of hunting crops.

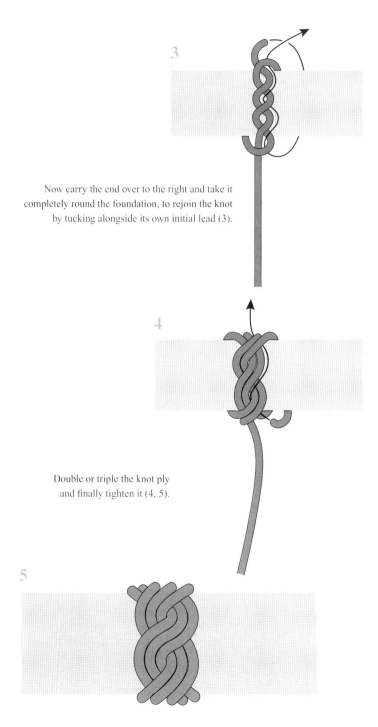

Now carry the end over to the right and take it completely round the foundation, to rejoin the knot by tucking alongside its own initial lead (3).

Double or triple the knot ply and finally tighten it (4, 5).

PRUSIK BOTTLE SLING

Carrying liquids in jugs, jars, bottles and carboys can be an awkward and arduous task. A sling lashed round the neck of any such container, with loops that act as carrying handles, is a labour- (and back-) saving trick.

Tie a basic bale, sling or ring hitch (1) in a knotted or endless sling or strop round the neck of the container to be carried.

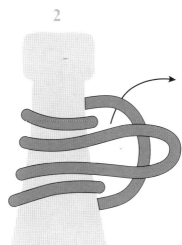

ORIGIN

The ancient Greeks and Romans used jar slings to manhandle their amphorae. Austrian professor of music Dr Karl Prusik invented the knot that bears his name in World War One; in 1931, he published instructions on using it as a means of self-rescue ascent for climbers.

Take the retaining bight round a second time and retuck it (2, 3). What results is the classic double Prusik knot used by climbers as a slide-&-grip knot.

3

Pull out the bight closest to the container once more, insert a half twist (4), and tuck the other bight through it (5). Tighten all of the turns, then tighten them again, before use.

4

5

However, this adaptation as a bottle sling was dreamed up by Dr Harry Asher of Birmingham, and first appeared in his *A New System of Knotting* (1986).

INDIAN JUG HANDLE

This knot has also been described as an Indian bridle knot, and is similar to hackamore knots (such as the Fiador or Theodore, *see pages 108–109*) that were used by Western American frontiersmen and women. See pages 178–179 for a brief outline of why and how jug, jar or bottle slings can be usefully employed.

Form an uncompleted overhand knot, then pull a bight through the loop to create a simple noose (1, 2).

Tuck the working end up through the pair of entwined knot parts, as shown (3), then take the end round behind the upper bight and tuck it down, from front to back, through its own bight.

ORIGIN
Dr Robert M. Wolfe, MD, of Chicago discovered the way of tying this knot that is illustrated here and let it be known in *Knotting Matters* issue no. 55 (March 1997), although the knot itself features in earlier mid-20th century knotting manuals as an Indian bridle knot.

Arrange the completed knot into a bracelet with one loop and two loose ends (4), then insert the neck of whatever is to be seized and carried into the central knot space marked X.

Tie the two ends together, having first inserted the longer one through the loop, to create a couple of self-equalizing handles (5).

LAPP-TO-STRAP

Wilderness pioneers, whether hauling sleds on Arctic expeditions or mending the worn harness of pack animals, as well as stay-at-home hobbyists of every kind, could usefully employ this simple method of joining a cord or rope to a leather or webbing strap.

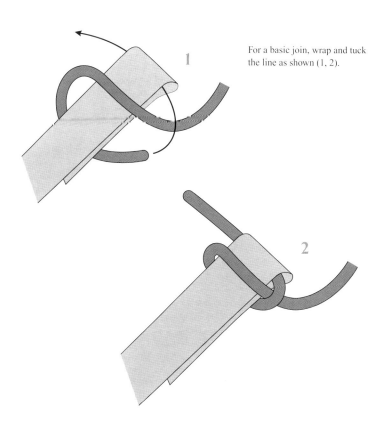

For a basic join, wrap and tuck the line as shown (1, 2).

ORIGIN

The Lapp knot tied as a joining knot in two lengths of rope or cord (*see page 76*) superficially resembles a sheet bend (and is sometimes called a 'false' sheet bend). This hybrid Lapp-to-strap was recommended in *Knotting Matters* issue no. 52 (April 1996) by Robert Pont.

183

Add an overhand stopper knot for added security (3).

To create an optional extra loop, bring the running end round to the opposite side of the strap and repeat the tying process (4, 5).

Pont reported that he had tested it in the worst of conditions, pulling heavy loads with the same knotted strap and rope over many months in sun, rain and snow, and had found it wholly reliable.

FALMOUTH CARRICK BEND

There are several carrick bends which, with their simple
forms (compared to some knots) and concentrated nip,
are suitable for joining cables and other ropes of large
diameter, although they work well in smaller cordage too.

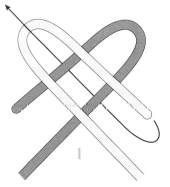

Form a bight in the end of each line and
lay one on top of the other, as shown (1).

Take the end that lies on top down and
round beneath its companion bight, then
tuck it up through itself (2).

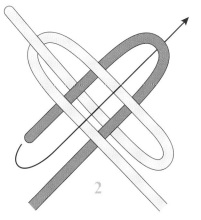

ORIGIN

This easy tying method was described
and illustrated by Owen K. Nuttall of
Huddersfield, in *Knotting Matters* issue
no. 23 (April 1988).

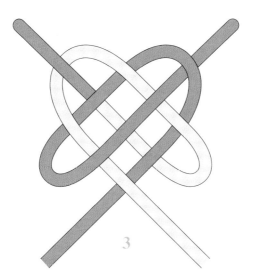

Similarly, take the end that lies
underneath over the top of the
developing knot and tuck it
down through its own bight (3).

Pull both standing parts in opposite
directions, then let the knot capsize
into its final form (4).

OPEN SESAME BEND

Here is another of those bends that consist of two interlocked overhand knots. It is a strong and secure specimen, which has the added advantage that tugging upon both short ends partially opens up the knot – hence its name – making it easier to untie.

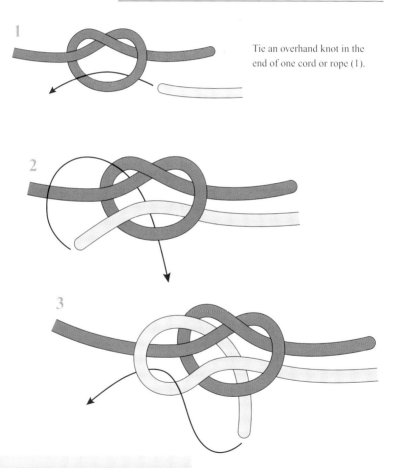

1 Tie an overhand knot in the end of one cord or rope (1).

ORIGIN
Dr Harry Asher discovered this knot, which he described in *Knotting Matters* issue no. 43 (April 1993). The name is a direct reference to the charmed words by which the door of the robber's dungeon flew open in the *Arabian Nights* tale of the Forty Thieves.

Insert the other end through the mouth or belly of the initial knot, then tuck and tie it as shown (2, 3, 4).

4

5

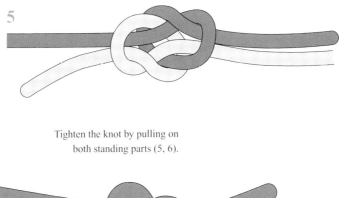

Tighten the knot by pulling on
both standing parts (5, 6).

6

COLLARED HITCH

This robust holdfast will withstand a steady or intermittent load from various directions, and may even cope with a longitudinal pull.

Lead the end round the foundation and behind its own standing part to create a sort of jacket collar (1).

Wrap again, in the opposite direction, and add a second collar opposing the first one (2, 3).

Now turn the work round, before bringing the working end over, from back to front, and inserting a locking tuck that goes over one, under one, over one (4).

Rear view

Methodically work the knot tight (5).

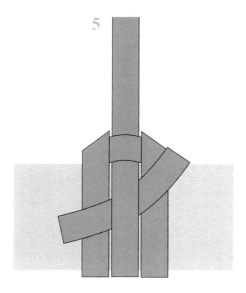

PIWICH KNOT

This reinforced version of a bale, ring, sling or hook
hitch is less likely to fall apart when the strain imposed
by the load slackens temporarily, and may also be slightly
stronger. There are two methods of tying it: when tied with
an end, that end ought then to be knotted to the standing
part of the webbing for complete security; when working
with a preformed loop, strop or sling, tying this knot in the
bight is the only available option.

Method 1: take the working end
over and down behind the point of
attachment, then bring it from right to
left (in this instance) across the front
of its standing part (1).

Take a turn with the end round the
standing part, before going behind,
over and down the front of the point of
attachment once more. Then tuck the
working end through the loop beside its
original lead (2) and tighten (3).

ORIGIN

This knot was reported in *Knotting
Matters* issue no. 47 (December 1994) by
Robert Pont of France, who first spotted
it in Quebec and kindly named it the
Piwich knot after the child whom he
witnessed tying it (Piwich Kust, of
the Bois Brule tribe).

Method 2: bend the top bight of the loop or sling down to create two loops, one (the left-hand one in this example) larger than the other (1).

Wrap the larger loop round behind and then bring it forwards, down over the smaller one, finally returning it to its own side (2).

Insert the foundation and tighten the knot (3).

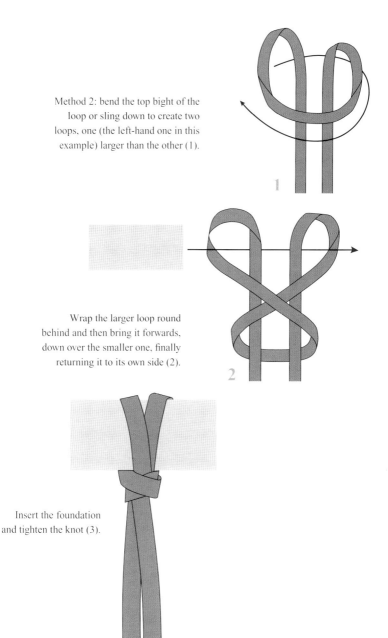

CHAIN STITCH LASHING

There is a continual need, whether aboard a smart sailboat or tidying one's garden shed, garage or closets, to lash together assorted items. This could take the form of furling unused sails in port or wrapping a rolled carpet for transportation. The chain stitch lashing will do the job, yet it may be cast off by pulling on one end, when it comes undone faster than a zip.

1

Start with a timber hitch (*see page 58*) and proceed with the long working end to make a bight (1).

2

Take the end round whatever is to be lashed and insert a second bight through the first one (2).

3

Repeat the process as often as
required by the length of both
package and available cord (3).

4

Finish off with at least two half
hitches (you can add one or
two more to be sure) (4).

VERSATACKLE

Few households possess a proper rope-rigged block-&-tackle, but this cleverly improvised alternative will apply (and multiply) tension wherever it is required. Tie it in small cord to clamp new picture frames, chairs or other woodwork while the glue dries; use it to hoist heavy loads or haul out a mired-in vehicle; tighten guylines and other standing rigging on tent, flagpole or mast. It really is a versatile tackle.

In one end of a long line tie a fixed-loop knot: the angler's loop (*see pages 68–69*) is ideal (1). Then, at a distance somewhat more than that of the points to be constrained by this tackle, tie a second angler's loop, so that the running end emerges from the side of the knot (2).

ORIGIN

This remarkable cordage contrivance first appeared in *Knotting Matters* issue no. 13 (October 1985), where it was described and illustrated by London inventor George Aldridge.

Now pass one end through the first loop, back through the second, through the first loop again and so on several times (3, 4, 5). Pull on the running end to exert a shortening force that brings the two loops closer together. Let go and it holds firm (although, for safety's sake, add a retaining half hitch or two). To release it, take out a turn or two from the loops, and loosen the entire arrangement.

PLAITED
INTERLOCKED LOOPS

Loops simply interlocked can in time weaken and even saw through one another. This arrangement spreads and minimizes abrasion, a function that can be invaluable in rope, cord or small stuff such as fishing line, as well as to its user's peace of mind (and wallet or purse).

Tie a fixed loop (in this instance, a figure-of-eight loop, *see pages 166–167*) in the end of one of the lines to be joined and twist three loops into it (1, 2).

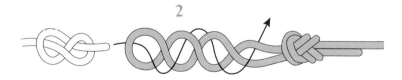

ORIGIN

This idea appeared in *The Hamlyn Book of Fishing Knots* by Geoffrey Budworth, published in 1999, and may have been his own invention.

Tie a loose figure-of-eight knot in the
other line, and then weave the free or
running end up and back through the
other line's loop, precisely as shown,
to create what is in effect a round
four-strand plait, like an
old-fashioned telephone cord (3).

3

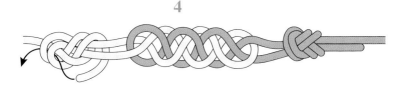

Complete the second figure-of-eight
loop and tighten the knot (4).

4

PLAITED LOOP

This elaborate fixed loop is a strong knot that, because
of its interwoven form, has an inherent elasticity which
absorbs some of the energy imposed by a shock loading,
and thus increases the ultimate breaking strength of the
line in which it is tied.

Arrange the line as shown, then
commence a three-strand 'pigtail' plait:
bring the left-hand strand over to replace
the centre one (1), then the right-hand
strand over to replace the centre one (2),
the left-hand strand over to replace the
centre one (3), and so on.

ORIGIN
This knot, called the Australian plait,
appeared in *Practical Fishing Knots*
(1991) by American writers Lefty Kreh
and Mark Sosin.

Repeat the process until the lower bight is only a little larger than the size of the required loop, then double the free or running end (4).

4

5

6

Wrap four or five turns round both bight legs, as shown, then pull on the end to eliminate the remaining small loop and tighten the seizing that has resulted (5, 6).

PLAITED SPLICE

This is a strong way to join two small lines – such as
fishing lines – and, as with the previous knotted loop, the
interwoven nature of the splice yields a degree of stretch
that will absorb at least some of the energy of a shock
loading, increasing the ultimate breaking strength.

Arrange the two ends of line to be
joined as shown (1), then begin a
three-strand 'pigtail' plait (2, 3)
(*see pages 198–199*).

ORIGIN

This splice was featured in the *Complete
Book of Fishing Knots & Rigs* by Geoff
Wilson, published by the Australian
Fishing Network in 1995.

As the working ends of both lines shorten, double the one that began as a collar round the other one into a bight (4). Continue to plait, treating the bight as if it were a single line, but imparting a half-twist for added neatness each time the bight appears as an outside strand.

When the bight is used up, tuck the other working end down through it (5) and trim both ends close to the completed splice (6).

FURTHER READING

From the hundreds of mainstream books and booklets about knotting that have been written since the beginning of the twentieth century, only a limited selection of those describing basic knotting has been listed below. These include a few climbing and fishing knot publications, for each of those pursuits enjoys a large following, but specialized topics – such as mathematical knot theory, the forensic analysis of knots and ligatures, rope splicing, netting, rigging, conjurors' rope tricks and macramé and other decorative knotting (for example, tying friendship plaits and Chinese knotting) – are not included.

Retail book stores either stock or can order many publications (including old titles, if they have been reprinted in an up-to-date format), although some will inevitably be out-of-print and must be searched for in secondhand bookstores or at car boot sales.

Adkins, Jan, *String – Tying it Up, Tying it Down*, 1992, ISBN 0-68418875-9

Asher, Harry, *The Alternative Knot Book*, 1989, ISBN 0-7136-5950-5

Ashley, Clifford W., *The Ashley Book of Knots*, 1944, ISBN 0-57109659-X

Berthier, Marc P.G., *The Art of Knots*, English translation 1977,
ISBN 0-356-08150-8

Bigon, Mario, & Regazzoni, Guido, *The Century Guide to Knots*, 1981,
ISBN 0-7126-0089-2

Blandford, Percy W., *Practical Knots & Ropework*, 1980,
ISBN 0-1806-9956-2

Bounford, Trevor, *Knots*, 2001, ISBN 0-00-710151-1

Budworth, Geoffrey, *The Ultimate Encyclopedia of Knots & Ropework*,
2000, ISBN 1-84309-138-0

Fink, Thomas, & Mao, Yong, *The 85 Ways to Tie a Tie*, 1999,
ISBN 1-84115-249-8

Gerber, Ham, *Making Discoveries in Knots*, 1990, ISBN 0-8323-0475-1

Goodhind, Wendy, *The Girl Guide Association Knot Book*, 1998,
ISBN 0-85260-146-8

Graumont, Raoul, & Hensel, John, *Encyclopedia of Knots and Fancy Rope
Work*, 4th edition 1952, no ISBN

Herzog, Bill, *Tying Strong Fishing Knots*, 1995, ISBN 1-57188-022-4

Hin, Floris, *The Colour Book of Knots*, 1982, ISBN 0-333-34164-3

Judkins, Steve, & Davison, Tim, *Knots & Splices*, 1998,
ISBN 1-8986-6-0476

MacNally, Bob, *Fishermen's Knots, Fishing Rigs, and How to Use Them*,
1993, ISBN 0-9646265-1-9

Miles, Roger, *Symmetric Bends – How to Join Two Lengths of Cord*, 1995,
ISBN 981-02-2194-0

Newman, Bob, & Knight, Tami, *Knots around the Home*, 1997,
ISBN 0-89732-207-X

Noonan, Michael, *Climbing Knots – for Lefties and Righties*, 1997,
ISBN 1-57034-053-6

Notley, Larry V., *Fly Leaders & Knots*, 1998, ISBN 1-57188-122-2

Pawson, Des, *Pocket Guide to Knots & Splices*, 2001, ISBN 1-85648-604-4

Raleigh, Duane, *Knots & Ropes for Climbers*, 1998, ISBN 0-8117-2871-4

Rosenow, Frank, *Seagoing Knots*, 1990, ISBN 0-393-03338-4

Sosin, Mark, & Kreh, Lefty, *Practical Fishing Knots*, 1991,
ISBN 0-71346993-5

Taylor, Roger C., *Knowing the Ropes*, 1989, ISBN 0-87742-970-7

Toss, Brion, *Knots*, 1990, ISBN 0-688-09415-5

Trower, Nola, *Knots and Ropework*, 1992, ISBN 1-85223-705-8

Warner, Charles, *A Fresh Approach to Knotting & Ropework*, 1992,
ISBN 0-959203-3-X

USEFUL INFORMATION AND WEBSITES

International Guild of Knot Tyers (IGKT)

The IGKT was established in 1982 and its membership is now approaching 1500. It is a UK-registered educational charity, but has a worldwide membership and is strongly represented in the United States. Members keep in touch by means of a members' handbook and a quarterly magazine, *Knotting Matters,* which contains informed articles, expert tips, letters, editorial comment and news and views about everything to do with knots. In the UK, IGKT members enjoy two major gatherings each year, but local groups (both in the UK and other territories) meet more frequently for lectures, demonstrations, and workshops. For further details (including subscription fees and an application form) contact Nigel Harding (IGKT Honorary Secretary) at: 16 Egles Grove, Uckfield, East Sussex, TN22 2BY, England. Tel: +44 (0)1825 760425; e-mail: igkt@nigelharding.demon.co.uk

IGKT websites

International Guild of Knot Tyers: www.igkt.craft.org
IGKT, North American branch: http://www.igktnab.org/
IGKT, Pacific American branch: http://www.pab.org/
IGKT, Texas branch: http://www.texasknot.tripod.com/

Animated knot-tying

Boatsafe, Stuart, Florida: www.boatsafe.com/kids/knots/htm

Boy Scout Troop 9, Billings, Montana: www.troop9.org/knots

Folsom's Knots and Knotting Page: http://www.folsoms.net/knots/

42 Brighton Scout Group, East Sussex, England:
www.mistral.co.uk/42brghtn/knots

Knot-tying and knotting links

Folsom's Knots and Knotting Page (50 useful knots, including some
animated ones, plus links and knot books, from Alan Folsom):
http://www.folsoms.net/knots/

Knots (knots for Scouts, with an index of about 130 common knots):
http://www.scoutingresources.org.uk/knots_index.html

Martin Combs (knot links and resources):
http://members.tripod.com/~knots/index-2.html

NetKnots.com (knots for camping, fishing and boating):
http://www.netknots.com

Peter Suber (comprehensive coverage and links under three main headings:
knot tying, knot theory and knot art):
http://www.earlham.edu/~peters/knotlink.htm

Ropers Knots Page (links to knot sites and an in-depth index of knots on
the Web): http://www.realknots.com

Scout Association of Australia (index of knots and lashings):
http://www.scouts.asn.au/knot_idx.html

Rope manufacturers and stockists

Brion Toss (American sailboat rigger and knotting writer):
http://briontoss.com

Jimmy Green Marine (UK chandler stocking ropes, rigging and safety
equipment): www.jimmygreen.co.uk

KJK Ropeworks (UK manufacturers of rope products and suppliers of
cords and fittings): www.kjkropeworks.co.uk

Liros Ropes Ltd (German manufacturer of synthetic and natural fibres for
yachting purposes): http://www.liros.com

Marlow Ropes Ltd (a leading manufacturer in the UK of sailboat ropes and
cordage): www.marlowropes.com

Rock-n-Rescue (Pennsylvania-based company supplying climbers, cavers
and rope-rescue teams): http://www.rocknrescue.com

Samson Rope Technologies (US rope manufacturer):
http://www.samsonrope/com

U-Braid-It Braiding Supply Co. (New Mexico mail-order suppliers of
plaiting materials for horse tack): http://www.ubraidit.com

INDEX

ACKNOWLEDGEMENTS

The author freely acknowledges the influence of all those earlier writers, illustrators and publishers who – through their numerous and varied books, booklets and technical manuals – taught him much of what he understands about knots. A great deal of their knotting knowhow reappears in this book, although considerable effort has been made to give a personal and, wherever possible, original presentation and spin to the data. Any preferences and prejudices that may be apparent in the contents (whether inspired or misguided) are the author's alone.

A special note of thanks goes to his editor Mandy Greenfield and illustrator John Fowler who, as key players in the Ivy Press's production team, were able, in mere months, to display a competence with the portrayal of knots that had taken him years to acquire.